HYLAN

the story of an Essex country house
and its owners

Stephen Foreman

IAN HENRY PUBLICATIONS

Dedicated to the memory of my father,
THOMAS WILLIAM FOREMAN, 1916-1976
and his five brothers -
Robert, Leonard, Reginald, Sidney and Dennis

2nd edition

ISBN 0 86025 492 5

Printed for
Ian Henry Publications, Ltd.
20 Park Drive, Romford, Essex RM1 4LH
by
Redwood Books,
Kennet Way, Trowbridge, Wiltshire BA14 8RN

Acknowledgements

The production of this book would not have been possible without the assistance of many people.

Firstly, Jane Dansie, the Essex County Local Studies Librarian, who wrote the script for the 1976 Chelmsford Arts Festival lecture on Hylands House, also Stan Jarvis for his encouragement in my local history research.

My thanks to the staff of the following; Chelmsford Library, Essex Record Office, Barking Public Library, Saffron Walden Library, House of Commons Library, Library and Drawings Collection of the Royal Institute of British Architects, Library of Writtle Agricultural College, Southend library, Hertfordshire Record Office, Gloucestershire Record Office, and to many other libraries and Record Offices who answered my letters.

The Rev B Davies, Rector of Widford, the Rev A G Willett, Vicar of Galleywood, and the Rev J B Potter, Vicar of Writtle, for permission to look through the parish records. I owe a debt to the British Red Cross Society (Essex Branch), Mrs Peggy Cash, the late Mr Harold Fairbank, OBE, the Girl Guides (Mid-Essex Division), Sir Robert D Gooch, the Great Eastern Railway Society, and Mrs L E Marshall.

My thanks to the many staff and officers of Chelmsford Borough Council without whose help over the years I could not have completed this book; in particular to Mr Graham Wade of the Parks Department, and Mr Esmond Abraham, the Borough Architect, who checked the details in the last chapter. I am also indebted, to Mr John Miller of the Architects Department.

If I have forgotten anybody's name it is not deliberate and I ask for his or her forgiveness.

Stephen Foreman - June 1990

2nd Edition

My thanks firstly go for the gracious permission of Her Majesty The Queen for allowing me to publish several letters from the Royal Archives at Windsor Castle.

Throuhghout the book various plates are reproduced with the kind permission of Chelmsford Borough Council. The park and estate particulars are repoduced with kind permission of Esmond Abraham, in addition, passages of text are from *Hylands: an architectural history*, which is the copyright of Esmond Abraham and Chelmsford Borough Council.

Again my thanks go to the staff of Essex Record Office and Chelmsford Central Library for their assistance, and to Nick Wickenden of the Chelmsford and Essex Museum.

My thanks also to Edith and the staff of Mablethorpe Library who have had to put up with my never ending stream of book requests.

To Doreen Otto and the Friends of Blue I thank for their correspondence about Meir's pottery of Hylands.

Stephen Foreman - December 1998

Hylands under restoration, 1988

INTRODUCTION

To the mediæval traveller the River Wid was one of the many obstacles in his journey. Slow and winding, it meanders to join the River Can near Writtle, where it broadens and it was here that travellers could ford the river safely. But to reach this point incurred walking several miles around a high piece of land that jutted across the valley and many people shortened their journey by walking across this high ground. No doubt this new route was exhausting and many a weary traveller stopped at the apex of the hill and, when rested, continued down into the wooded valley that lay before him, with the hamlet of Chelmsford in the distance. It was from this hill or 'high land' that, no doubt, the present name derived. The track was soon to become established as a road, one of several that ran from the London road to Writtle and one of which was to form part of the boundary of the Hylands estate.

Between 1100 and 1111 Maurice, Bishop of London [d.1107], had a bridge built over the River Chelmer, enabling the inhabitants of Chelmsford to cross into the nearby hamlet of Moulsham. According to Philip Morant's *History of Essex* of 1768, this bridge 'brought the road that lay through Writtle this way; and gave some increase to the town, by the resort and benefit of travellers'. But even he did not fully realise the importance that this bridge was to have on Chelmsford and the surrounding countryside; while Chelmsford grew and thrived, Writtle's importance began to dwindle.

The earliest mention of Hylands, as it is now spelt, can be traced back to the reign of King John. In 1204 a manuscript relating to forest boundaries tells that the old Roman road from London to Chelmsford was called a 'noble causeway' in conjunction with Hylands. It reads -

Beyond the causeway towards the north which leads from Stratford towards Colchester, as far as the wood of Wildhora where at the head of the ditch called Haydiche it is joined to the aforesaid causeway and from thence beyond the causeway as the wood extends to the new bridge and from whence as the highway extends as far as Heighlands.

In documents from the reign of Henry III it was called Hoiland. It is thought that Hylands was part of the estate owned by Richard de Montfichet who, when he married a young widow named Jacosa, brought with her this piece of land as part of her inheritance from her first husband, Thomas D'engaine. Little is known of their life; Richard died in 1268 on the Crusades and Jacosa in 1274. They had no children to inherit the estate and so it was distributed among the children of his three sisters.

Although there have been several stories of 'large important mansions' on the site, there is no historical evidence to substantiate these claims, probably it was one of the many fields anonymously ploughed through the ages by the local inhabitants.

On 10th September, 1500, Thomas Hawkin, yeoman of Writtle, died, leaving in his will several parcels of land to the church, as well as building two almshouses. The endowment consisted of a house called Hooks and a number of fields, one called Highlands. The entire income from the bequest was to be used by William Carpenter, Vicar of Writtle, for the benefit of the poor dwellers in the almshouse near the church, except for four shillings and four pence that was to be placed at the disposal of the Vicar for praying for the souls of Hawkin and his family.

It was the manor of Shaxstones, in which Highlands Field was situated that was to emerge from the estate of the Montfichet family and was to be owned by many families. In the 16th century it was owned by William Bedell and in the 17th by Sir Andrew Astley and his heirs and, later, by the Brown and Roger families. Eventually it came into the hands of John Plomer, yeoman of Chislehurst in Kent, who owned the manor with his brother. In 1723 it was occupied by John Judge and, sometime thereafter, the estate was sold by John Plomer before his death in March, 1726, to a young Essex lawyer.

The new owner of the Shaxstones estate was to bring changes and it is therefore with this man that the story of Hylands really begins...

THE COMYNS FAMILY

JOHN COMYNS [OWNER 1728-1740]

For somebody who described himself as being 'not ambitious of honour or riches' and 'whose sole ambition hath been to do what good I could in my passage thro' ye world', the new owner of Shaxstones was to reach the heights of *noblesse oblige*.

John was the eldest son of William and Elizabeth Comyns and was probably born at his father's estate of Rollestones, Writtle, being christened at Writtle Church on 18th February, 1668. John Comyns was educated at Felsted School under the prolonged headmastership of Mr Christopher Glascock: Felsted was, in the 18th century, the centre of education for all the chief families of the county. From there he went on to Queen's College, Cambridge. He was to follow a strong family tradition by entering the legal profession and so entered Lincoln's Inn on 5th May, 1683. On 15th May, 1690, law studies completed, he was called to the Bar and soon won himself a reputation for legal learning, rather than for any special brilliance.

On 21st April, 1693, he married Anne Gurdon, daughter and co-heir of Dr Nathaniel Gurdon, Rector of Chelmsford, and, in 1697, on his mother's death, he inherited a small town house called Guy Harlings in New Street, Chelmsford, which his father had bought in 1675. He lived there for many years within a stone's throw of his father-in-law's church.

Most of the larger and ambitious Boroughs of the 18th century engaged an eminent lawyer or, preferably, the local Member of Parliament to fill the position of Recorder and many a prominent barrister's son was to rise in society. John was appointed Recorder for the Borough of Maldon's courts, thus introducing him to the inhabitants of the town where he was to make his first steps in politics. Charles Montague, Lord Halifax [1661-1715], persuaded John to stand for Parliament and, much against John's own inclination, he was eventually to stand as candidate in the 1701 election as John was 'violently opposed to ye then ministry'. In the reign of Queen Mary II, when he expected better treatment, 'I was by every

3

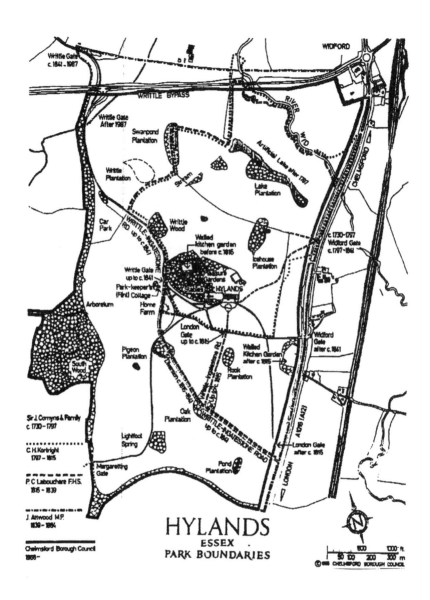

HYLANDS
ESSEX
PARK BOUNDARIES

ministry successfully treated with disregard, not to say despight, tho' I was not conscious of giving any just offence.' He was immediately elected Member of Parliament, continuing to represent it as a Queen Anne Tory until 1708. He was one of the first members of the Society for the Promotion of Christian Knowledge in their foundation year of 1698. His promotion in the legal profession was increased when, on 8th June, 1705, his Serjeant's coif was conferred.

His wife, Anne, died on 28th February, 1705, and was buried in Writtle church. He doubtless threw himself into his work and his eminence in the legal profession was to increase in 1706 when he was made Serjeant-at-law and he travelled the courts of the Home Circuit from 1706 to 1726.

John continued his association with Felsted School; at the second of the School feasts, held in 1708, he, with Charles Tyrrell, held the post of Steward.

He re-married on 20th October, 1708, to Elizabeth Courthope, and was re-elected the Tory M.P. for Maldon from 1710 to 1715: on 24th January, 1715, he declined to take the necessary oath and so lost his seat on petition on 20th May, 1715. His 'for want of a qualification' was to lose him his parliamentary seat, which went to Mr Samuel Tufnell. The qualification required was for an income of £3,000 per annum in real estate, as stipulated in the Qualification Act of 1711; as a result he was discarded by almost all the Tories. John was later to recall that his Parliamentary career had for many years reduced his earnings and, in a letter to Lord Hardwicke, he noted that he was able to 'go quietly on in my business till I gained by my practice about £3,000 a year'.

In 1719 he was in a court case at Chislehurst, Kent, as Counsel for the Defence: it was a case outstanding only in its absurdity. A London clergyman and the trustee of a charity for orphans, went to Chislehurst and preached a chantry sermon to raise funds - and was accused of vagrancy. John Comyns lost the case and the clergyman and trustees were all fined six shillings and eight pence.

At Lord Raymond's importuning John was to re-enter politics and it is certain that by 20th March, 1722, he had

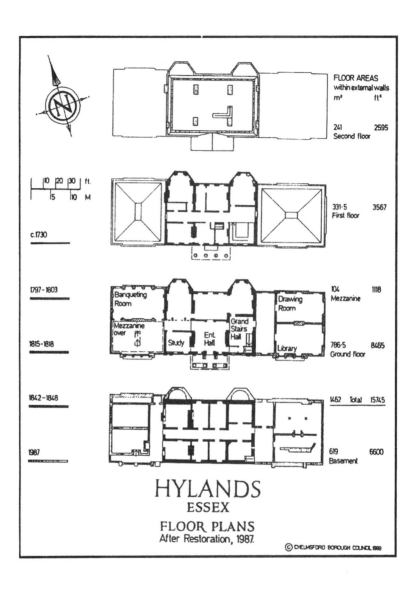

FLOOR AREAS
within external walls
m²	ft²	
241	2595	Second floor
331·5	3567	First floor
104	1118	Mezzanine
786·5	8465	Ground floor
1462	15745	Total
619	6600	Basement

c.1730

1797-1803

1815-1818

1842-1848

1987

Banqueting Room

Drawing Room

Mezzanine over

Grand Stairs Hall

Study

Ent. Hall

Library

HYLANDS
ESSEX
FLOOR PLANS
After Restoration, 1987.

obtained the necessary property qualification and was again elected Member for Maldon until 25th January, 1729, despite a petition by Henry Parsons against him. On 4th November, 1726, he was made Baron of the Exchequer (£1,500 p.a.), the next day he was knighted. Among his many friends and possibly the manipulator of his knighthood was the Prince of Wales, the future King George II, to whom Sir John was a counsellor. As a result of his extra responsibilities Sir John decided not to stand for Parliament again.

It was a dream of Sir John's to have a grand country seat, so befitting his family's place in society. Guy Harlings, a small town house in Chelmsford, was quite unsuitable for his new social standing and, so while he and his wife resided there, the search for a suitable residence was started. The ideal home would, of course, be newly-built in the latest style, but to do that one required land on which to build.

The Manor of Shaxstones at Writtle was up for sale. Consisting of about 170 acres of land, an orchard, a garden with 27 crofts and two meadows, this estate would meet all Sir John's requirements. It was near his father's estate, it was within a few hours ride of his old parliamentary seat at Maldon; and it was close to the main road to London. The farmhouse was of timberframe construction and not at all suitable, so a new building was to be built on a section of the estate that lay to the south of the farm, consisting of pasture land and woods. This house would show all the latest design and elegance of the period, a source of envy for all the local gentry - its name 'Hylands'.

Hylands House, of which only the core now remains, was built between 1728 and 1730. Earlier, in 1725, Sir John Comyns had commissioned the English architect, John James [1672-1746] to survey Serjeant's Inn on behalf of the Dean and Chapter of York, from which Sir John had characterised James as 'a person of unquestioned skill and fidelity', but there is no further connection between Sir John and John James.

It is also possible that Sir John may have met Giacomo Leoni [1686-1746], a Venetian architect, who, from 1728 to 1744 was working on Benjamin Mildmay's house, Moulsham

Hall. It is documented that John visited at least once, on 20th December, 1734, and it is possible that Leoni would have been staying there at the time. But the one date in 1734 is insufficient proof.

In a copy of the *Chelmsford Guide*, dated about 1807, it mentions that Hylands was planned and executed under the direction of Sir John Comyns and, in documents dated 1740, it quotes that Hylands was 'lately built by him'. Which architect was employed by Sir John is unknown. It is possible that Sir John used one of the many books that were published: William Halfpenny, Batty Langley, Inigo Jones and other architects of this period all produced books on architecture, which were a sort of do-it-yourself design-your-own-house instruction book, full of illustrations, plans, etc. So possibly it was built by local craftsmen, such as the Hillyard and Horsenail families of Writtle, who were known to have been working during this period as bricklayers and carpenters.

When the boundary of the land was established around the hundred acre estate, it was enclosed with a wooden fence. The grass and paddock were tended and the ploughed fields were turned into rich pasture. An old English formal geometric garden was laid out adjacent to the East Wing. A pleasure garden was made to the north of the house and a small greenhouse was built to serve the house with fruit and vegetables.

The estate was separated from the main London-Chelmsford road by an adjoining field and a driveway from a side road leading towards Writtle was used to provide a new gateway leading to the house, with a circular turn-around in front of the house. A second gate at the northern extremity of the estate gave access to the village of Widford.

An engraving of about 1770 clearly shows that Hylands itself was a small country house, characteristic of the Queen Anne period. Constructed of red brick adorned with white stone quoins and window dressings, seven bays wide and two storeys high, its the central three bays were flanked with pilasters carrying a central pediment containing a circular window. A pitched roof with dormer windows lighting the attic area was concealed behind a parapet wall.

The layout of the rooms had six on the ground floor, possibly an entrance hall with staircase, a billiard room, a study, a drawing room, a library and a dining room. The first floor had eight rooms, bedrooms and boudoir. The attic area was doubtless used for the benefit of the serving staff, but no details of domestic offices attached are known. The light wells surrounding the basement of the house were protected by a wrought iron balustrade.

Little is known of the internal decoration; it may be assumed that it did not have any of the more ornamental decoration that it was to have in later years. The only exception was the study where pine panelling was fitted below a heavy cornice. Virtually all traces of Sir John's 'neat and modern built house' have been submerged under later alterations, though a survey of the building has revealed that wallpaper was used at some period during Comyns' time.

After Sir John and his wife had established their new home to their liking, Sir John turned his thoughts towards the poor and needy and, on 30th September, 1731, he conveyed to the Churchwardens and Overseers of Chelmsford a piece of land near New Street, for the benefit of the nearby alms-houses. On 22nd May, 1732, he was made governor of Chelmsford Grammar School and he was to progress further in his legal career by replacing Sir Thomas Reeves [d.1737] Justice of the Common Pleas on 5th January, 1736.

The pinnacle of his career came on 8th July, 1738, when he became Chief Baron of the Exchequer (£2,000 p.a.), in place of Lord Chief Baron James Reynolds [1686-1739], who had resigned his position and retired, but this triumph was marred by the death of his wife, Elizabeth, in the October and, though he was to marry for a third time, to Anne Wilbraham from Cheshire, he was not to be blessed with a surviving heir.

A typical court case of the time is shown in a chronicle of July, 1740; it tells of Mary Richardson and Sarah Gibbs, spinsters, being sentenced to transportation by Lord Chief Baron Comyns and Baron Lawrence Carter [1672-1745] at the Chelmsford Assizes for stealing a gown from Margaret Rounce at Chadwell Heath.

On 13th November, 1740, Sir John Comyns died at the age of 73. He was greatly missed, not only by the local gentry, but more particularly by his many friends and colleagues in the legal profession. Lord Chief Justice William Draper Best [1767-1845] said of him, "We cannot have a better authority than that eminent writer," and Lord Lloyd Kenyon [1732-1802] said, "His opinion alone was of great authority since he was considered by his contemporaries as the most able lawyer in Westminster Hall".

In Sir John's will he left the Hylands estate to his nephew, John Comyns of Pettits, Romford, on the condition that his 'Lady for life' (widow) could continue to live the rest of her life there, should she so wish. Lady Anne lived at Hylands until about 1745, when she moved to Blunts Hall, near Billericay, where she stayed until her death on 10th June, 1758.

The Chief Baron was dead, but he was not forgotten, his good works lived on after him. Poor clergymen in Essex could remember him as they enjoyed the benefits of a trust fund that he had established on their behalf. The inmates of Writtle workhouse could thank him for leaving money so that their governor could read morning and evening prayers to them.

There are two paintings of Sir John that survive. One is by Arnold Houbraken [1660-1719] and belongs to Lincoln's Inn, now in the Courtauld Institute, London; the other is in the style of the school of Sir Godfrey Kneller [1646-1723] and in Valence House Museum, Dagenham.

JOHN COMYNS [OWNER 1745-1760]

John Comyns was the eldest son of Sir John's brother, Richard and his second wife, Frances. John was educated at Queen's College, Cambridge, and followed the family tradition by entering the legal profession. In 1718 he was admitted to the Inner Temple and in 1724 was called to the Bar; later, on 5th February, 1730/1, he was to enter Lincoln's Inn.

In December, 1727, he married Isabella Wright, who died in October, 1738. On 23rd May, 1740, he re-married, to Elizabeth, second daughter of James Hallet, of Little Dunmow,

The bust of Sir John Comyns by Sir Henry Cheere in Writtle Church

John Richard Comys and his family, by John Greenwood

Yale Center for British Art

in St Paul's Cathedral. On his uncle's death that November he inherited Hylands and all Sir John's legal papers.

The fame that Sir John Comyns attained as a great lawyer was to increase greatly after his death when his works, two books on law, were published. The first, produced in 1744, was his *Reports of Cases adjudged in the Courts of King's Bench, Common Pleas and Exchequer* and covers the cases Sir John was involved in from 1695 to 1740. John had studiously translated Sir John's papers from 'law French' into English and the publication was publicly acclaimed by many great 18th century lawyers and statesmen.

John's love and affection for his uncle must have been considerable, as Sir John's work on *The Digest of the Laws of England* was started upon after his *Reports* were finished; by 1822 it was in its fifth edition and expanded to eight volumes.

In May, 1747, John Richard Comyns, the eldest of John's sons, entered the world, but more of him later. The Comyns suffered great grief on the death of their two-year-old daughter, Mary, in 1751.

John progressed to Master of the Bench, Inner Temple, in 1754.

Elizabeth died in May, 1756, and on 11th November that year John married his third wife, Mary, sister of Sir John Tyrell. On 8th July of that same year he was awarded his Doctorate of Civil Law.

In 1759 John commissioned the eminent English sculptor, Sir Henry Cheere [1703-81] to commemorate the life of Sir John and so a fine rococo monument was placed over the family vaults in Writtle church; the main sarcophagus has carved supporting legs standing on a plain plinth, on the front is an inscription, while on the lid are the sword and scales of justice and a fine bust of Sir John flanked by two urns. Behind was formerly a tall obelisk-shaped panel with his shield of arms, but this was removed in 1950 when the church window was opened up; it is now in the South Porch.

On 6th October, 1760, John died, leaving his estate to his son, John Richard. The Essex historian, William Holman [d.1730], in his manuscript notes for a history of Essex describes John as a 'gentleman of great hopes and likely to prove an ornament to his profession'.

Alas, John did not see another of his great dreams realised; Sir John's *Digest of the Laws of England* was not published until 1762, some two years after his death. Though both of Sir John's works were amended, altered and added to over the following years, it must be said that, were it not for John's translations, two great legal works would not have been published. By 1792 the *Reports* were republished by Samuel Rose, who added in his preface that its 'publication was demanded by the legal profession' - no greater tribute could have been given.

JOHN RICHARD COMYNS [OWNER 1760-1797]

John Richard was born in 1747 and inherited Hylands in 1760 while at the tender age of 13. He was educated at Magdalen College, Cambridge, matriculating on 16th January, 1766. In an accounts book of 1765 a Martin Yorke, overseer of the parish of Widford, was rated as occupying Hylands: he was probably leasing it from the young John Richard, while the latter was at college.

John Richard married Elizabeth Brackenbury at Widford church on 8th January, 1770, and on 12th October that year the first of his three daughters was born. In 1768 John Richard conveyed the advowson of Beauchamp Roding and other property to William Birch in order to provide an annuity for John Comyns' widow, Mary, and in 1770 sold the same advowson to the Rev Richard Birch of Roxwell and John Birch of Boswell Court, London.

The loss of a family dog prompted this advertisement in the *Chelmsford Chronicle* of 6th December, 1776:

Chelmsford, December 5th, 1776

Lost

From Hylands, near Chelmsford in Essex, about the 12th of last month. A Dane dog, sully spotted with black, his ears cropped and answers to the name of Spot, had on when he went away, a leather collar with a brass plate, the inscription thereon "John Richard Comyns Esquire, Hylands, near Chelmsford in Essex". Whoever will return the said dog to the printer of this paper may receive five shillings reward, and all other reasonable expenses.

The American artist, John Greenwood [1727-92], was commissioned to produce an oil painting of John Richard with his family, seated in one of the rooms at Hylands. The painting, dated 1775, is now in the Yale Center for British Art, Connecticut.

Crime in 18th century Essex was rife and in the *Essex Chronicle* of 13th March, 1778, an advertisement was placed:

Whereas the stable door and garden gate of J R Comyns, Esq. at Hylands, near Chelmsford, were broken open on Thursday the 5th instant, and several things stole out of the garden; notice is hereby given, that Mr Comyns intends every night to set spring guns and traps in his gardens, shrubbery and other parts of his premises. Mr Comyns hereby offers a reward of five guineas to any person who will give information of the offender, or offenders, to be paid upon conviction of such offender or offenders.

But Hylands was a large undertaking to run and so it seems that John Richard decided to sell a number of pieces of property, including the family town house of Guy Harlings, which was sold to John Badeley in 1785.

In a series of weekly advertisements in the *Chelmsford Chronicle* from 31st July to 11th September, 1795, Hylands itself was put up for auction:

An excellent mansion, and most desirable residence, and freehold estate in Essex, to be sold in a short time by auction. The capital house, called Hylands. Beautifully situated between the 26th and 27th milestones, on the west side of the high road from London to Chelmsford, in the occupation of John Richard Comyns, Esq. (the proprietor) being a handsome, uniform, substantial, and well built brick mansion house, three stories high, containing six rooms on the ground floor, and eight on the second floor, with good attic, and all convenient offices, a greenhouse, ice house, gardens and pleasure gardens in a paddock of 100 acres, well wooded and watered. Also, the meadow or Grass Farm, and demesne lands, adjoining; together with the capital or manor farm called Shackstones, and other lands, on lease to Mr Robert Crances, containing in the whole 400 acres, all freehold, and lying together in a ring fence, in the parishes of Widford, Writtle and Chelmsford. Further particulars, and tickets for viewing the premises every Wednesday and Saturday, between the hours of eleven in the morning and three in the afternoon, may be had by applying to William Birch, Esq., 54 Dean Street, Soho, London, (and John Oxley Parker, of Chelmsford, where plans of the estate may be seen).

For the first time an accurate description of the house is known, giving a few bare details of the house and the surrounding estate.

In an advertisement of 13th October, it was announced that the sale was postponed until the spring of 1796. In the *Chronicle* of 11th March, 1796, it said that the auction would be held in the May or June unless disposed of by private contract. The final notice of auction was in the *Chronicle* of 26th August, 1796.

Freehold Mansion House, lands and farm, Essex.

To be sold by auction by Messrs Skinner, Dyke and Skinner.

On Tuesday, 20th September, at 12 o'clock at Garroway's Coffee House, *Change Alley*, Cornhill, in one lot. A valuable and very desirable estate, most agreeably situate on an eminence and extending to the highroad; two miles from Chelmsford, in the county of Essex, and twenty-seven miles from London, called

Hylands

with the manor or reputed manor Shackstones, Shackstones Manor Farm and Bridge Farm.

Hylands Mansion House is a commodious uniform residence, with all proper offices, coaches houses, stabling, pleasure grounds, gardens and park, or paddock, which together with the farms contain near 400 acres of meadow, pasture and arable land, well wooded, refreshed by rivulet and within a ring fence.

Shackstones Farm, containing 230 acres, is in the possession of Mr Robert Crances, on lease for a term of 17 years at a rent of £220 per annum. With other beneficial reservations.

Remainder consisting of Mansion House, offices, gardens and park, and Bridge Farm are in hand, of which immediate possession may be had.

To be viewed twenty days preceding the sale and printed particulars had on the premises; also of Messrs Clachar and Co., Chelmsford; the Cock and Bell, Romford; of William Birch, Esq. Dean Street, Soho; the place of sale; and of Messrs Skinner, Dyke and Skinner, Aldersgate Street, London, where a plan of the estate may be seen.

John Richard seems to have moved out of Hylands by this

time for some reason, and so it was not until the early autumn of 1797 that a buyer was found.

An advertisement for the sale of household goods was placed in the *Chelmsford Chronicle* on 26th May, 1797.

Sale of Furniture

To be sold by auction,

By Clachar, Meggy and Chalk,

On Tuesday the 30th May instant, and following day,

(On the premises)

The household furniture, and other effects, at Hylands,

In Widford, near Chelmsford, Essex;

Consisting of four post and other bedsteads, with printed cotton, moreen and other hangings, window curtains, goose beds and bedding; drawing room suites, bureau and bookcase, chests of drawers, a set of mahogany dining tables, 14ft 6in long by 5ft wide; dining, tea, Pembroke, writing, and other tables; elegant pier glasses in gilt and other frames; variety of sofas; marble and other side-boards; large Wilton and other carpets; fire screens; wine cellarets and coolers; handsome mahogany billiard table, complete; a barrel and finger organ, in wainscot case 8ft by 4ft; an excellent 8 day clock in a mahogany case; variety of kitchen, dairy, and brewing utensils; a pleasure boat; a 3 hogshead brewing copper; washing ditto; wagon, two dung carts, ploughs, harrow, a taxed cart, coach harness, plough traice, a chain pump, three stone garden rolls, a carriage for breaking-in horses, a Yarmouth cart, a lead cistern, and a variety of other articles, which will be expressed in catalogues, to be had three days previous to the sale, at all the inns in the neighbourhood, at the place of sale and of the auctioneers, Chelmsford.

Also about 14 loads of meadow hay.

Sale to begin each day at half past ten o'clock.

John Richard moved to Burstead Lodge, Billericay, but he lived only a few months and died of the gout on 5th October, 1798; his remains being placed in the family vault in Writtle church. Elizabeth, his wife, was to live until 20th February, 1826, when she was laid to rest next to her husband.

CORNELIUS HENDRICKSON KORTRIGHT
[OWNER 1797-1814]

Cornelius was born around 1763/4, his family being of Dutch origin. He was married to Juliana Margaretta, the daughter of Major-General Waltersdorff of the Danish Army. Cornelius owned several large estates in the West Indies, many on the island of St Croix, then under Danish colonial rule. Little is known of his early life, although we know his first three sons were born in Santa Cruz and Porto Rico. It is probable that he was one of the owners who grew rich from the lucrative slave trade or that of growing sugar. There are indications that at least one distant member of the Kortright family had been a privateer, *i.e.* a pirate with letters from his government authorising his piracy. He decided to return to civilisation to live in luxury, his decision no doubt being hastened by Denmark's 1792 decision to make slavery illegal.

After a short stay as guests of the Whishaw family at Aston House, Hertfordshire, where his daughter, Maria Newton Cornelius, and a black slave, John Bastain, were both baptised on 22nd October, 1796. The surname Bastain was long associated with the family name of Kortright. Cornelius bought the entire estate for the sum of £14,500 and moved into Hylands House in the summer of 1797.

The Romantic Movement was sweeping England and all the notables of the country were taken with the idea of landscape gardening and of this new style of architectural art, which was merged with the style of the Neo-Classical or Greek Revival. Cornelius must have been enthralled with the new fashion and so, between the autumn of 1797 and 1803, the entire estate was to be transformed by one of the foremost landscape gardeners - Humphry Repton [1752-1818]. The profession of landscape gardening had gained considerable prominence during the 18th century and he was engaged to sculpt the park and to enlarge the house to allow Cornelius' ever-increasing family to live in comfort.

Repton, from his home in Hare Street, Romford, set to work. Little of the building work that Repton was to design still exists, but we do know details of some of his embellishments. John Preston Neale's engraving of Hylands in 1819* shows Repton's Corinthian tetrastyle portico being built on the front, extending the original pediment by ten feet and supported on four Ionic columns to form a portico with an inner panelled roof. This masked the entrance hall, which had a dentilled cornice and was flanked by arched windows. Plain single storey extensions were added to the west and east of the building with saddle backed roofs five bays wide, the centre three having Ionic centre columns and the windows double sashes with glazing bars. The east wing had a bow-windowed drawing room and a south facing conservatory; the west wing housed the servants' quarters and stabling. Repton disapproved of red brick buildings, preferring them to be covered in white stucco. In the basement were eight large wine and beer cellars, the basement light wells were filled in and the ground levels around the house regraded.

On the ground floor one entered the marble paved entrance hall 24 feet square, off which was a geometrical stone staircase and a back staircase, a billiard room 19'6" by 15 feet, a study 19'6" by 15 feet, a drawing room 23 by 18 feet, a dining room 28 by 17 feet six inches, a new extension to the south of a large drawing room 40 feet by 22'6" with a ceiling 18 feet high, and a conservatory and aviary 43'6" by 12 feet ran parallel to it, also, a wardroom 19 feet by 7'6".

The west extension was shorter and wider and was probably a refaced service wing that was already existing; contained within were housekeeper's rooms, butler's pantry

* Neale was an architectural draughtsman, who had an original sketch turned into an engraving by J Wallis. With the assistance of Edward W Brayley, who wrote the descriptive text, he produced the first series of six volumes of *Views of the seats of noblemen and gentlemen in England, Scotland and Ireland* in 1819. This was followed by a second series of a further five volumes published between 1824 and 1829. The view of Hylands House is from the second volume of series one and is clearly dated 1st March, 1819. It is a little known fact that the proliferation of county histories produced at the turn of the 19th century, together with the engravings of views and country houses, palaces and notable residences of the landed gentry, greatly assisted one of Britain's growing industries.

Humphry Repton,
print by
William Holl
after
Samuel Shelley

Chapman & André's map of Essex, 1772

and room, water closets, larders, large servants' hall, kitchen, scullery and coalhouse.

The curved bay windows on the garden side were added at this time; they are clearly shown on the 1814 map, but do not appear in the cellar and so are unlikely to be from the original house.

On the first floor were six large bedrooms, three dressing rooms and housekeeper's closet; they were probably unaltered since the house had been built. The attic does seem to have been changed and now contained two large bathrooms with dressing rooms, a large nursery and five other bedrooms. The alterations to the attic may have been done in December, 1797, when it was reported in the local paper that Mr William Polley, who was by profession and plumber and glazier (a trade used for laying a lead covered roof) had fallen some thirty feet from the roof; luckily he landed on some hollow boards, so saving his life. He had, it seems, thought that he had put his foot on some straw that had been laid on the parapet roof by bricklayers, as was the practice of the time, but unfortunately there was no roof underneath the straw.

A weather vane, dated 1798, was erected on the roof, possibly to commemorate the occasion and was still in position well into the 1950s, but has since disappeared. It is a shame that it could not have been put back on top of the house now renovation has taken place.

Other domestic offices near the house included a large laundry with a bedroom over it, a wash house and a brewhouse.

Repton had the final results of his work published in an engraving dated May, 1804, in Peacock's *Polite Repository and Pocket Companion.* The engraving was the work of J Peltro, but it was based on an original drawing of Repton's which he did at the completion of each of his commissions. Repton usually required two or three day's work, during which time he would probably have stayed at Hylands as a guest. The charge for his design was usually between six and forty guineas.

His survey would have entailed the use of a theodolite, the making of notes both written and sketched and the taking of measurements. He would have studied the house thoroughly and walked or ridden over every acre of the estate; he would probably have visited the home farm and the nearer of the farms that were let to tenants. In the course of conversations with Cornelius he would have made sure either that his patron was prepared to put himself entirely in his hands and understand roughly what this would cost; or that, had he ideas of his own, there would be a workable measure of agreement between the two as to what should be done and what the likely cost was to be.

Repton would have left him when he had all the material he needed and, in due course, perhaps a month, perhaps three months later, he would have returned to stay for a day or two again, to present Cornelius with a *Red Book*, one of over two hundred he was to have made for each of his commissions by the year 1803.

The *Red Book of Hylands* would, like all of them, have been a slim volume measuring 13½ inches by 8½ inches, handsomely bound in red or brownish-red leather - hence its name. These slim volumes in their morocco bindings were intended to lie on library tables, to be shown to admiring friends, and thus discreetly to advertise their creator's skill, thereby engendering further commissions.

A red book consisted of delightfully prepared small water-colours bound together with his manuscript recommendations. They often had movable flaps attached, so as to give the effects before and after his proposals had been carried out. The text was usually divided into short sections under headings such as Character, Situation, Approaches and Water. The introduction tended to be somewhat obsequious in tone and there was generally a flattering reference to the client's good taste or ideas, which Repton doubtless found to be a safe way of ensuring a favourable reception for his own recommendations.

Alas, the present whereabouts of the *Red Book of Hylands* is unknown: it seems to have disappeared from the house sometime after 1839. It must be either destroyed or left unrecognised amongst the possessions of a past owner or servant as an extensive search of libraries and museums has failed to uncover it. Certainly it has not come up for sale at any of the larger auction houses. And so it must, unless anyone knows better, remain a loss to architects and gardeners alike who now, while the house and park are being renovated, would like to consult the master plan of this time.

Repton did write and publish books on gardening; in his *An inquiry into the changes of taste in landscape gardening*, published in 1806, he quotes:

The comfort and pleasure of a country residence require that some ground, in proportion to the size of the house, should be separated from the adjoining ploughed fields; this enclosure, call it park, or lawn, or pleasure ground, must have the air of being appropriated to the peculiar use and pleasure of the proprietor.

And in his *Observation on the theory and practice of landscape gardening* of 1803:

A form so generally adopted in modern houses, that I will not mention any particular instances, especially as they are in the works of living architects; yet I hope I shall be pardoned in also making some observations on their construction.

This last invented form consists in a compact square house, with three fronts, and to the back are attached offices, forming a very long range of buildings, courts, walls, &c, supposed to be hid by plantation.

These I have been often required to hide by planting, while, in fact, during the lives of the architect and the proprietor, the buildings can never be concealed, and in the lives of their successors the trees must be cut down to give a free circulation of air to the buildings.

In 1803 in his *Theory and practice of landscape gardening*, he specifically mentions Hylands by name; he spelt it Highlands:

The operations of landscape gardening have often been classed under the general term of improvement; but there are three distinct species. The first relates to places where the grounds are altered and adapted to a house already existing; the second to those where the houses, by additions, having changed their original character, or aspect, renders it necessary to make alterations in the ground also; the third includes those places where no house previously exists, and where the entire plan of the house, appendages and grounds, has sometime been called a creation. Among the second may be mentioned those, in which the entrance of the house being changed, new rooms being added, or barns, stables, and kitchen-grounds removed, new arrangements have taken place, as at Highlands, Brandsbury, Holwood, etc.

The gentle rolling meadows and cultivated landscape of Hylands were clearly to his liking and a number of features that Repton encouraged are known to have taken place there. These include surrounding the park with belts of trees and thinning out of some of the larger groups of trees; adding the artificial canal to the north of the estate and adding trees around it to enhance its size; building a kitchen garden near the house; adding a ha-ha around front of the house; adding drives around the pleasure garden, usually of six feet wide with two feet of grass borders, the drive usually constructed of gravel; altering the front drive, eliminating a circular bed in front of the house and altering the routes of the drive to the Widford gate; eliminating Comyns' small garden made when the extension to the east of the house was made; pulling down and rebuilding a group of buildings, probably stables, servants' quarters, etc.; extending the area of the park as a whole down to the River Wid, including the construction of a walled garden containing a greenhouse to the north of the house; building a lodge at the park entrance near Widford; excavating a deep lake in the pleasure garden, possibly to provide clay to make bricks for the extension to the house; and, providing an ice house to the north of the house, located near a lake, so that, in winter, large blocks of ice could be cut and placed in a partially underground building so as to give a cold atmosphere for the preservation of food.

Who actually executed the heavy work of landscaping the park is unknown, possibly some of the gardeners, and no doubt a large number of local workers were employed for the heavy digging work that was required. One gardener at Hylands was William Ranciman, whose son, John, was baptized at Widford church on 22nd February, 1806.

One happy Christmas must have been that of 1801, when Cornelius' father-in-law, Major-General Waltersdorff, arrived on Christmas Day at Hylands House.

Crime was prevalent in the Comyns' time and was to continue with the new owner. It was reported in the

Chelmsford Chronicle of 19th September, 1800, that Hylands was attacked -

On the night of 12th September, Hylands, the seat of C H Kortright, Esq., was attacked, the butler having fortunately discovered that some persons were about to break in, fired a blunderbuss from the window, on which the villains decamped to the back part of the house and, on endeavouring to enter, were overheard by the gardener, who fired a brace of pistols, which deterred the depredators from proceeding in their intentions.

Crime certainly did not pay in those days!

The Chelmsford races, held at Galleywood, were a local attraction and Cornelius was Steward for the races in 1800.

Once all the alterations had taken place a tranquil aura settled over the estate. In 1802 Cornelius swapped land near Widford bridge for an equal area with Mr Benjamin Surry and the Turnpike Trustees agreed to rebuild the bridge, which was greatly in need of repair; but the bridge collapsed completely on 8th February, 1805, to be rebuilt using cast iron beams.

Between 1803 and 1815 Cornelius was Churchwarden at Widford. He raised a new breed of sheep, being a cross between the Merino and South Down, being very fine in their wool and parties from the local agricultural society were shown them. In January, 1808, a twenty pound reward was offered in the *Essex Herald* for information leading to the arrest of persons who had wilfully cut and destroyed several young fir trees near the lodge gate at Hylands; possibly this was the destruction of some of Repton's work.

During the Napoleonic Wars Chelmsford's Barrack Square and the new heavy fortifications built at Galleywood overlooking the Wid Valley, meant a large number of military personnel being based close by. One such person was General Sir George Whitmore [1775-1862], who held the rank of Captain-Lieutenant in the Royal Engineers and was posted to the Eastern District to assume the command of the Engineers' Department from April, 1803 to 1811. His headquarters were at Colchester Barracks and he was responsible for the fortifications, not only at Galleywood and Widford, but also the many Martello Towers along the Essex-Suffolk coastline, including the large Redoubt at Harwich. The fortifications at

Galleywood/Widford were thrown up by military working parties, the left flank was secured by a stone redoubt at Widford and, on the right, by a stronger work on Galleywood Common, passing through the park - as it was called - of Sir Henry Mildmay. It was whilst engaged on this work that he took the opportunity to paint two small watercolours of Hylands. It is not know for certain whether Cornelius and the young Captain-Lieutenant met socially. Certainly, they had subjects in common, including the fact that George was based in the Caribbean from 1800 to 1802. George recorded that he had visited the island of St Croix and other islands as part of his military service. The two watercolours, dating from about 1803/4, are now in the Gloucestershire Record Office.

The *Essex Herald* of 23rd January, 1810, reported that:

On Tuesday last Mr Kortright gave an elegant ball and supper at his beautiful seat Highlands, near this town, at which all the fashionables in the neighbourhood were present, including many military gentlemen. About one hundred sat down to the supper tables, which were covered with every delicacy of the season, after which dancing was kept up till daylight appeared the next morning.

By 1814 Cornelius had put the estate up for sale and resided at a smaller house at Fryerning called Maisonette, a few miles south. The sales description of the estate was even more detailed than that of 1797 -

Hylands, in the County of Essex.

To be sold by private contract, with immediate possession.

A remarkably elegant modern and substantial mansion house, delightfully situated on an eminence, at a desirable and convenient distance from the turnpike road leading from Chelmsford to London, with suitable offices of every description, calculated for a family of the first distinction, together with about 213 acres of fertile meadow, posturing and woodland, laid out as park and pleasure grounds, beautifully interspersed with flourishing and ornamental timber and shrubberies and watered by a handsome canal at the bottom of the park, within view of the house, and commanding beautiful and extensive prospects of the surrounding country; and to which a bailiffs house and farriery is attached. Also the Manor or Lordship, or reputed Manor or Lordship of Shackstones, with the rights, royalties and appurtenances thereof; and about 371 acres of extremely rich fertile, arable, meadow and pasture land consisting of

John Richmond's clock in the stable block

Part of the servants' quarters

three compact farms, called Shackstones, High Elms and The Lodge, in the several parishes of Chelmsford, Widford and Writtle. Shackstones and the Lodge farms, containing about 210 acres, are under a lease to a particular good and respectable tenant, whereof 11 years were unexpired at Michaelmas next.

The Mansion house contains in the basement, 8 large and excellent wine and beer cellars; on the principal or ground floor, a paved entrance hall, 24ft square, communicating with a principal geometrical stone staircase and a back stair case. A handsome Billiard room, 19ft 6in by 15ft; study, the same size; Drawing room 26ft by 19ft 6 in; Library, 23ft by 18ft; Dining room, 28ft by 17ft 6 in; large Drawing room 40ft by 22ft 6in, and 18ft high, opening into a beautiful conservatory and aviary 43ft by 14ft; wardrobe adjoining, 19ft by 8ft; housekeeper's rooms, butler's pantry and room, water closets, larders, large servants' hall, and a most excellent kitchen, scullery and coal house.

On the principal bedroom floor are 6 large and excellent bedrooms, and 3 large dressing rooms, admirably disposed, and a housekeeper's closet. In the attics are 2 large bedrooms, with most convenient dressing rooms, a large nursery, and 5 other bedrooms. The domestic offices are of the most complete and convenient description, comprising a large laundry, with bedroom over it, a wash-house, brew-house, etc.

In the stableyard are 3 coach houses and a chaise-house; harness and saddle rooms; wood house, coal-house, granary, and potato house.

The gardens of the mansion house are walled in with high walls and tastefully laid out, and well stocked with the choicest fruit trees in their prime of bearing; and contain gardener's house, pinery, hot-house, etc. and conveniently situated, is a very good ice house.

The above farms are contiguous to the park; and the whole estate (except 4 acres) freehold, and exonerated from land tax and forms a most desirable investment.

The roads are remarkably good; the country well stocked with game; several packs of hounds are kept in the neighbourhood; and coaches to and from London pass the lodge of the park-gate almost hourly: distant from London 27 miles - from Chelmsford, 2 miles.

Any person wishing to become the purchaser of the mansion house may be accommodated with any part of the estate and farms he shall desire.

The estate may be viewed, and price and particulars known, on application (if by letter post-paid) to C G Parker, Esq., Chelmsford, at whose office plans of the estate may be seen; and the price and particulars may be also ascertained from Richard Van Heytheyson, Esq., 12 John Street, Bedford Row, London.

As well as his house at Fryerning, Cornelius also owned a town house in Mortimer Street, London, but it was while on a visit to Cheltenham that he died, aged 54, on 27th September, 1818, and was buried in Fryerning churchyard. His wife, Juliana, died at Mill Green House, Fryerning, in December the following year, aged 50.

Engraving of Hylands by J Peltro, after a drawing by Humphry Repton, 1804
Chelmsford Library

PIERRE CAESAR LABOUCHERE [OWNER 1814-1839]

Pierre-Caesar Labouchere was born into a Protestant family that had its origins in the small town of Orthez, in South-west France. His father, Mathieu de Labouchère [1721-1796], was a cloth merchant. The Labouchères were one of many families to flee France after the revocation of the Edict of Nantes in 1685. Though not one of the first families to leave, they were amongst those who were to seek a new life elsewhere. Many fine artisans set up new homes in London and Essex during this period, as a result of this emigration.

During the early 18th century, Mathieu moved to the safe haven of Holland, and set up house at The Hague. He married his first wife, Anne Elizabeth de Courcelles, in 1748: their only son Henrie Pierre died young. By 1769 he had re-married, to Marie Madelaine Molière [1742-1825], who gave birth to four sons and two daughters.

Their second son, Pierre Caesar, was born on the 2nd November, 1772, and baptised five days later.

It was in the prosperous trading ports of Amsterdam, Antwerp and The Hague that the young Pierre assisted his father in his business. With the Dutch East India Company set up in 1602 and the West India Company in 1621 Holland had the political and financial backing that was to rival that of their only real competitor - London. The 19th century economist, Adam Smith, said that in Holland "it is unfashionable not to be a man of business". Mathieu sought employment for Pierre, and in 1790, he entered the service of the merchant banking firm of Henry Hope & Co as a clerk.

In 1794 French revolutionary troops invaded Flanders and pressed onwards into Holland and, with the Dutch military in disarray, The founder of the firm, Henry Hope and his son, John William Hope, left Holland on 17th October, 1794, to set up their banking empire in England.

They left Pierre in charge of the firm, with powers of procuration, and the management of affairs was to rest solely with him. Pierre and Alexander Baring [1774-1848], the son of Sir Francis Baring [1740-1810], who was serving his apprenticeship at Hopes, were now trapped by the invading French troops, their getaway being hindered by severe frost, many rivers being jammed with ice. Crossing the North Sea was now impossible and it was not until 18th January, 1795, that they were able to embark at den Helder for England and safety, just as the French troops entered Amsterdam.

The Baring family was to welcome the Hope family to England, and this was to start a long association between Baring's and Hope that lasts to this day. Pierre was one of the most talented bankers of his generation, gaining valuable experience throughout Europe whilst on company business. It was on one such visit to England that he fell in love with Dorothy Elizabeth Baring, the daughter of Sir Francis Baring. He asked Sir Francis for his permission to marry and was refused. He then asked if Sir Francis would change his mind were he to become a partner in Hope's and was told that he would. So he immediately returned to Amsterdam to ask the Chairman of Hope's if he would make him a partner; again he was refused. He then asked whether it would influence the decision if he knew that he was engaged to the daughter of Sir Francis Baring, the owner of the biggest and richest bank in England: it certainly would! Whereupon Pierre wrote a letter reminding Sir Francis of his promise.

With such daring and initiative a marriage such as this was bound to be a success and so they were wed on 26th November, 1796. The spirit of the story lives on, but the true facts do not bear it out, as he was not to become a partner in Hope's for several years.

Pierre was soon to be seen all over Europe. He was short on wit and education, but his generous nature, combined with a sense of honour and an acute knowledge of banking matters, made him a figure akin to that of a pre-Revolutionary French aristocrat. He spoke English with a French accent and his native French with an English accent.

By 1797 England was in deep financial trouble and, in the following years, Pierre was to travel the breadth of Europe: in April, 1798, to Hamburg to settle the outstanding repayments of Martin Dorner.

With the Treaty of Amiens in 1801 peace existed in Europe and Pierre journeyed to France and, later that year, to Portugal on a mid-winter mule journey across the Pyrenees, in the company of George Baring, concerning a large diamond loan. Pierre was to complain that the Portuguese 'constantly alter the text, and 1 have to puzzle my brain to find out in a language which I do not understand the right from the wrong'. The loan initially for 6.5 million guilders was to increase to 13 million, but it was not the financial success it was envisaged.

Eventually the Laboucheres were to return to Holland on 10th October, 1802, but the peace did not last very long and hostilities between France and England broke out again in May, 1803.

When the purchase of Louisiana from France by the United States of America was mooted Pierre was deeply involved in the negotiations. Largely due to Pierre, a successful agreement was signed on 2nd May, 1803, whereby Barings and Hope's were to purchase Louisiana from France and re-sell it to the United States for a sum totalling over US$27M for an area of nearly 830,000 square miles, which would, in a single stroke, double the area of America.

James Monroe, who had been involved in the negotiations, had married on 16th February, 1786, Elizabeth Kortright [1768-1830], the daughter of a British ex-Army Officer. It is my belief that Cornelius Hendrickson Kortright was a close relation, but the exact relationship has yet to be confirmed - possibly her grandfather or her grandfather's brother, both who are known to have to come to England to live. Therefore it is a distinct possibility that James and his wife may have visited such a close relative either in London or at their home - Hylands. In 1817 Monroe became fifth President of the United States of America.

Dorothy Labouchere, who suffered from rheumatism, took the waters at Bagnères in France, and, while returning from there, suffered an attack of fever.

In 1810 Pierre was involved, via a favourable approach from Louis Bonaparte, in a peace mission with France. On this mission Pierre was to be accompanied by Louis' Foreign

Minister, Willen Frederik Roell. Pierre sailed from The Brill on 2nd February, 1810, landing at Great Yarmouth on 5th and arriving in London the next day. However, nothing was to come of these negotiations.

In June, 1811, Pierre left for St Petersburg; this was to be the first of several trips over the next few years, when he was eventually to meet Czar Alexander [1777-1825] in 1813. Passports were handwritten at this time and one, dated 12th March, 1812 was personally signed by Napoleon, the Minister of Police and the Secretary of State. Pierre set off for London in January, 1814, probably meeting Czar Alexander, who was then making a state visit to England.

The 584 acre estate of Hylands was put up for sale in October, 1814, and was a convenient residence for Labouchere, offering the advantage of being just outside London for privacy and having ease of access to the east coast ports for travel to Europe. The sum of £40,000 was conveyed to C H Kortright from the trustees of Dorothy Labouchere, via Baring Brothers & Co, £8,000 being used to discharge an existing mortgage and an additional £7,750 for the nearby estate of Stisted.

Alexander Baring, Pierre's companion in Amsterdam twenty years before, was to become his next-door neighbour, as he moved into Cut Throat Hall, a short journey from Hylands.

It was said that the 'Alliance Loan' of Barings in Paris in 1816 doubled Pierre's fortune and, in 1821, he decided to settle permanently in England, leaving his brother Samuel in charge of the House of Hope. In 1823 he resigned as a partner in Hope's and lived on the fortune he had accumulated, although he continued to dabble in monetary matters.

Many historians have credited the architect William Atkinson [c.1773-1839] with having built the two single storey wings to Hylands, but it is clear that they were not his but those of Humphry Repton. Atkinson did construct several buildings in the park, as well as some minor work to the house between 1819 and 1825. The curved bay windows of Repton were to be altered to straight sides, thus forming a half-hexagonal shape and the portico was rebuilt to a much larger size. The servants' quarters were removed and a matching

P C Labouchere
William Atkinson
Flint Cottage

symmetrical west wing with a mezzanine floor was erected. The house was now complete, with its great unfluted Ionic style portico and colonnades in antis setting off the wings.

It is not known for sure who was employed to do some of this work, but certainly it was done at the same period as Atkinson's work. New stables were constructed on which a clock tower, the mechanism being made by John Richmond of Springfield, Chelmsford, was perched. Homestead Farm was built of the same red brick and a kitchen garden was moved to the east of the estate. A new London gate was built on the high road as the estate was extended to the south.

The greenhouse was replaced with a much larger erection of some 250 feet long with Portland stone flagstones and heated with cast-iron hot water pipes - it was a magnificent sight. Atkinson had been given the honour of being the first inventor of a practical apparatus for heating greenhouses; his system used an open-topped boiler with a movable cover and two pipes connected to the top and bottom of the boiler running to an open topped reservoir, later using a closed top to the boiler, it could carry hot water some thirty feet above boiler height. The pipes were usually laid around the sides of the greenhouse, near the floor or sunk into the floor and covered by a cast iron grille. This was a great improvement on earlier, but unsuccessful, boilers. Possibly the greenhouse at Hylands contained such a system and would be at the forefront of the development of hot houses; the great glasshouses, such as Kew and Chiswick, were not built until the 1830s.

Flint Cottage may have been built by Atkinson, possibly as an extension to his early experiments with the use of flint. He published in 1805 *Views of Picturesque Cottages* and mentioned his recent, successful experiments with the material. It is not known for sure when the land on which Flint Cottage was built became part of the Hylands estate. The cottage has now lost its thatched roof, replaced at the start of this century, and Chelmsford Council demolished a later extension that was affecting the main structure; today it is in poor condition, boarded up and put to no practical use.

To accompany the external redecoration the internal

Plaster cast of Aurora by Bertil Thorvaldsen

The glasshouse in the pleasure garden

decoration of the house was to be transformed. With the early 19th century neo-classical style still the rage, Pierre and his son, Henry, became collectors of many pieces of art in this style. The most highly regarded of the artists of this period was Bertel Thorvaldsen [1770-1844]; although Danish, he spent virtually all his working life in Rome. Among the commissions were several for Pierre, most of which still survive, either in the house or subsequently sold.

These included a pair of roundels in the entrance hall at Hylands, one of several plaster cast copies of the relief that was modelled in 1815 in Rome.

Some modern critics have observed that these graceful roundels, which Thorvaldsen took less seriously than his larger works, were his most successful creations: these included 'Day carrying the genius of Light, Hesperus', showing Eos or Aurora scattering the roses of the Dawn, carrying on her back the Genius of light, Hesperus, the torch-bearing child; 'Night with her children, Sleep and Death' of marble, Nyx, the winged female figure, crowned with poppies, bears in her arms the twin children, Sleep (Hypnos) and Death (Thanatos); also a frieze in the staircase hall at Hylands; 'The Triumphant entry of Alexander the Great into Babylon', a plaster cast copy of a panel from the Quirinal Palace, where an expected visit by Napoleon in 1812 was commemorated by a commission by Thorvaldsen and a reduced version was executed by his pupil Pietro Galli [1804-1877] in 1822. The present position of this frieze, in what was the original Georgian staircase, suggests that it may have previously adorned one of the principal rooms in Labouchere's house, which was either re-modelled or demolished by a later owner, John Attwood.

Items no longer in Hylands House are a bust of Sir Henry Labouchere, first Lord Taunton [1798-1869], modelled in Rome and executed in marble in 1828, probably commissioned by Pierre as a reward for his son's successful completion of his university examinations; 'Venus Triumphant after the Judgement of Paris', sculpted in Rome 1813-16, commissioned by Pierre and eventually received in 1829. This was delivered by sea in the hold of a sailing ship that was ill-fated; of the three Thorvaldsen statues that were on board ship, one was smashed, one lost an arm and Pierre's Venus, whilst being hoisted from the hold, slipped and fell back, luckily the accompanying cargo of wheat cushioned the fall and Venus suffered no damage.

On Pierre's death it was inherited by his son, Henry, and it is now in the Thorvaldsen Museum in Copenhagen.

Two other dispersed items are 'Vulcan forging the Arrows of Love', a marble relief acquired by P C Labouchere through Alexander Baillie, executed in Rome 1814-15, and in Stoke Park, now a golf club house at Stoke Poges, at one time Henry Labouchere's home; and 'The Ages of Love', acquired directly in Rome by Pierre as a graceful apology for the delays in completing 'Venus', in the Danish Embassy in London.

In the *Chelmsford Chronicle* of 23rd February, 1824, an advertisement was placed:

"Whereas a black greyhound dog became a stray, near a month ago, to Hylands. Any qualified person owning the same may have him again by describing his marks and paying the expenses, on application to Joseph Furmedge, Gamekeeper, Hylands, Widford.

He is a very fine handsome and doubtless a valuable dog, and if not owned within one month from the date hereof, he will be disposed of, to defray the charges."

In 1828 an account was read to the (now Royal) Horticultural Society of London by John Smith, gardener at Hylands. It reported on the growth of cherry trees and the possible remedy for their protection against bird attack when the fruit is approaching maturity. He said that, in 1821, a cherry orchard was planted near the pleasure gardens at Hylands by William Atkinson from designs Pierre had brought back from his travels across the continent. This innovatory construction consisted of a covered area of one rood and twelve perches and was surrounded by a 9 feet high wire fence of 2 by 1 inch mesh and a number of posts suspending fishing nets that were specially made at Bridport, Dorset, completely covering the orchard. Ninety-eight cherry trees, many of them May Dukes, White Hearts and Circasrain, as well as gooseberries, red, white and black currants, raspberries and strawberries were grown, safe from the hungry bird population.

Ladies and gentlemen could wander about and help themselves from fruit trees and bushes.

The political cartoonist, George Cruikshank [1792-1878], produced an etching in 1826 called 'Exhibition extraordinary in the Horticultural Room'; amongst the figures portrayed is Pierre, but it is not known for sure which character he is portrayed as.

In March, 1828, the *Gardener's Magazine* published an article explaining the Dutch manner of forcing. The gardeners, Francis Nieman, who looked after vegetables and fruit, and John Smith, the flower garden and pleasure gardens, showed the reporter the kitchen gardens and talked of their methods of growing, but without meddling with the theory of gardening. Mr Nieman had been brought from Holland especially to look after the gardens. They substituted dung heat for fire heat and used leaf mould instead of loamy soil, with reed mats for covering. Hot bed frames measuring 9ft 6in by 6ft 3in wide, each frame having two sashes; those intended for lettuces divided into 30 squares, for other crops 42 squares, the top and bottom, sides and side styles being of wood. Glass was put into leaden laps with four iron rods inside for added strength. The panes were 10 by 11 inches for lettuce and 10 by 9½ inches for other purposes, the box or frame being 18 inches at the back. Mr Nieman had several M'Phail's pits for use. On 7th November, 1827, there were 13 lights, each containing 30 plants of lettuce. Mr Nieman said he would cut lettuces every day until May next, the variety seems to have been like Union Cabbage Lettuce.

Melons and cucumbers were prepared in January or February and harvested in September, cucumbers being cut every month of the year, and the first melons being cut at the beginning of May. Carrots and radishes were made on an old melon bed, the first sowing being made in the last week of September; along with other sowings in the hotbeds there were six or seven sowings in the open. No carrots of a large size were ever used by the Labouchere family, except by the servants! The type seems to have been a good variety of the Early Horn.

Kidney beans were sown in an old melon bed prepared in the last week in August and needed a good deal of heat. A bed composed of fresh dung was made in the second week of November for the second crop, which came into bearing in about six weeks, that is, about the first week of January. The type was Small Early White, a hybrid between Dutch Runner and Early White Dwarf. Cauliflowers were made on a bed of half spent dung, made in the last week of December and grew little until February; they were eventually cut in April.

Peas were still to be gathered in the open air and he had a quantity in full bloom: were November a clear month, he might gather a dish in the first week in December. He usually gathered the first peas in April; the type appeared to be Early May.

Potatoes, asparagus, sea-kale, tart rhubarb, chicory, parsley roots, mint, tarragon and other herbs were also grown.

Pits for peaches, apricots, vines and raspberries measured 8ft 6in wide, being surrounded by a brick wall 5ft high and 4ft in front, the back walls being between 1 and 2 feet higher than the front. The first crop of peaches, nectarines and apricots were placed from the last week in November to the first week of January. The third crop was obtained from large greenhouses built by Mr Atkinson. From fan trees, covering 10 square feet, Mr Nieman gathered 150 fruit. The first apricots were usually ripe at the end of April or the beginning of May, the peaches and nectarines in the second week of May.

Cherries of the type May Duke were frequently, and plums, apples and cherries occasionally, forced.

The second crop of peaches was brought forward in low steep-roofed greenhouses 25ft long, 8ft wide and 8ft tall in the highest part, the back and front walls being of brick. The brick wall had trained cherry trees and a pit for strawberries of the type Roseberry and Red Alpine.

Vines were the type Dutch Sweetwater and Frankendale of the Hamburgh variety. One vinery for early forcing was fitted with a hot water system under the direction of Mr Atkinson. Raspberries of the type Red Antwerp seem more suitable for forcing that white.

Reed walls and screens used by Mr Nieman were imported from Holland, as they were stronger than British reeds. Locally made mats were from Mr Robert Resker, reed mat manufacturer of Writtle, who made mats to any size at a penny farthing per square foot.

Such was the success of his gardening that on 25th May, 1832, the Horticultural Society of London awarded Pierre the Banksian Medal for his exhibit of forced apricots, raspberries, melons, &c., and on 10th May, 1834, the Silver Banksian medal for forced apricots and raspberries. Pierre also exhibited at the Chelmsford Horticultural Society's shows.

The peaceful existence of the estate was to be interrupted. The new-fangled railways were coming and Parliamentary sanction for a line from London to Norwich had been given in 1836. The Eastern Counties Railway Company planned to build the line through part of the Hylands estate; at Thorndon Hall, near Brentwood, the home of Lord Henry W Petre [1820-1889], the threat was exactly the same and so Pierre and Lord Petre joined forces to stop the destruction of their estates. They were served with notices informing them that some of their land was required for the track. Their cases were very similar, each maintaining that:

The construction of the railway according to the route described would ruin the house as a family residence, the privacy and retirement of it. The construction would make such an inroad upon his lordships pursuits upon his estate and of his enjoyment thereof... that he must certainly seek a residence elsewhere.

A provisional agreement was reached by which the railway company was to pay Pierre £5,000 for the value of the property taken and £30,000 as compensation for injury to his estate. But before the appropriate Act of Parliament was passed, the company's financial advisors sent surveyors to check the facts and figures and to report their findings.

Their report recommended that Pierre should receive only £4,000 and added that they considered the railway would not be at all objectionable and, indeed, would be of great benefit to his estates, thus enabling Pierre to travel to the Metropolis faster than by carriage, as well as enabling vegetables, etc., to be sent to markets, in London.

Whilst this wrangling over the railway continued, Pierre went on expending large sums of money on his house and estate and 'his benevolent hand distributed comfort and content amongst the cottages of the surrounding poor'.

His counsel in financial matters was held in great esteem and respect by those who knew him and Hylands was the frequent resort of many distinguished foreigners, including the celebrated French statesman, Charles-Maurice de Talleyrand-Perigord [1754-1838], the then French Ambassador to Britain, who was his guest for a time.

During the hard winter of 1837/8 a list of ligneous plants that survived the rigorous snows was published in the *Gardener's Magazine* by J A Ferguson, the gardener at Hylands.

In early January, 1839, Pierre was taken ill with a ruptured blood vessel; he began to recover after a few days, but on Wednesday night, 16th January, he was suddenly taken ill again. Despite the timely appearance of Dr Holland, physician to the Duke of Sussex, Pierre was to die at 11 o'clock that night. His body was conveyed to Over Stowey in Somerset, where he was interred in the family vault.

The procession was followed to the entrance on the London road by about 20 of the domestic staff; at the entrance to the park at the lodge about 30 gardeners and labourers were ranged on each side of the carriage road to allow the mourners to pass between them.

He had left two sons, Henry [1798-1869], the Master of the Mint, who later became Lord Taunton, and John Peter [1799-1863], an eminent London banker.

Henry inherited the estate, including outstanding legal problems, the matter of the railway not having been settled yet. When Henry came to assessing the estate he concluded that the inconvenience suffered through the railway had been less than initially feared. He therefore wrote to the Company relinquishing £15,000 of his father's claim. As the railway company was on the point of bankruptcy this gesture was well received. Owners of Hylands were now able, according to the Eastern Counties Railways Act of 1838, to plant shrubs and trees on the embankments and to hunt vermin; the railway company was to mow the grass not more than twice a year. The line from London to Chelmsford was completed in 1843.

John Peter was married in 1830 to Mary Louisa DuPré; they had a son, Henry DuPré Labouchere, who became famous, if not notorious, as a radical Member of Paliament and journalist, known to one and all as 'Labby'.

In 1839, Henry decided to put the estate up for sale in one lot at an asking price of £80,000. The whole estate containing some 750 acres altogether was auctioned on Friday, 19th July, 1839, and was advertised in the *Chelmsford Chronicle* that month:

Mansion, Park and farms,
In the county of Essex.
To be sold by auction,
By Mr Hoggart,
At the Mart, on Friday, July 19, 1839, at twelve, in
One lot, by order of the Executors,
Hylands.

The beautiful Mansion and property of Peter Caesar Labouchere, Esq. deceased situate at the 27th milestone from London to Chelmsford, adopted for the immediate reception of a family of distinction.

Embracing a domain of about 750 acres of rich arable, meadow, pasture, and park lands including the several farms of Shaxstones, High Elms, and the Lodge with Hylands. The mansion is placed upon a fine elevation, presenting two fronts, at a distance from the road, embosomed by stately oaks and plantations, approached by three entrance lodges, commanding the most extensive and beautiful prospects of the surrounding country, and replete with every accommodation; there are 22 sleeping rooms, several dressing rooms, ladies boudoir and water closets; on the principal floor is a dining room, 35 feet by 18; billiard room, 25 by 21; breakfast room, 24 by 20; splendid library and drawing room, 43 feet by 23 feet, and 14 feet high, opening to a conservatory and a glazed verandah.

The entrance-hall is 25 feet by 24, with house keeper's room, still room, butler's rooms and office of every description, most perfect in arrangement. The principal rooms have all double sash windows solid mahogany doors, and marble chimneypieces.

Detached is a substantial building of uniform elevation, forming a square, with spacious inner court-yard in which are six coach-houses, stabling and boxes for nine hunters, and standing for nine carriage houses, saddle and hamess-rooms, grooms and coachman's bedrooms, lofts, &c. complete.

The lawns and shrubberies, with which this delightful residence is surrounded, are intersected with gravel walks, branching off in various directions to the flower garden, which is celebrated for the high order and neat condition in which it has always been kept. The magnificent conservatories and stove houses are filled with a very choice collection of rare plants and exotics, and the hot houses and frames with grapes, peaches, nectarines, apricots, strawberries and raspberries, all growing in perfection.

The whole of the building having lately undergone the most thorough and substantial repair, may be kept up at a very moderate expense, and the garden establishment may be extended or reduced according to the wishes of a purchaser. Attached is a cherry orchard of considerable size, surrounded by a wire fence, and covered in by netting, as well for the protection of the trees as to prevent birds from injuring the fruit. There is also a great acquisition to this beautiful spot in an establishment of hot and cold baths, the latter being copiously supplied from a never failing spring of the purest water. In short, the limits of an advertisement cannot do justice to all the merits of this favoured spot. The farms attached to the property are in the occupation of Robert Robertson, Esq. under the highest state of cultivation and condition, and of which possession may be had in October next, with an excellent farm residence, adapted for a gentleman's occupation, with an arrangement of all useful and requisite farming buildings, in complete repair. The principal part of the park and estate is enclosed with oak park paling, a considerable portion new within the last year. The particulars when printed will enter into a more detailed description of this property.

The mansion and estate can only be viewed with particulars, which may be had at one shilling each, twenty-one days before the sale, of Messrs Lawfords, Solicitors, Draper's Hall and of Mr Hoggart, 62 Old Broad Street, Royal Exchange, London. Particulars will be forwarded to the Black Boy, Chelmsford; White Hart, Brentwood; The Cups, Colchester; and for special permission to view, application must be made to Robert Robertson, Esq., of Shaxstons.

When it came to the sale of the furniture and art objects

on 19th July, there was a great crowd eager to buy items from Pierre's magnificent collection of *objets d'art* he had accumulated over the years during his forays abroad. Possibly it included a library of 10,000 books purchased by Pierre in 1812 for 350,000 francs from Prince Charles-Maurice Talleyrand-Perigord. It was even said that an agent from Albert, the Prince Consort, was there to buy several items.

The *Chelmsford Chronicle* had for several months been running a series of articles on 'Homes of the Essex Gentry' and included Hylands in their edition of 19th July, 1839.

Homes of the Essex Gentry

Hylands

The seat of the late P C Labouchere, Esq., Hylands cannot now in strictness be ranged with our Homes of the Essex Gentry, for its master has passed from the gay saloon to the cold sepulchral marble - even the voice of grief has passed away - the splendid hall is comparatively desolate - and the stranger wanders through the study and the boudoir; but still we are induced to take a hasty glance, at its beauties ere they are passed, perhaps broken up and scattered, by the magic hammer of the auctioneer.

The mansion has no lingering remnants of antiquity about it. We see around us all the full ripe fruit of the present, unmingled with the crisp and dead and dying blooms of the past. Yet if it be true, as the historian tells us, that Widford, which rises before us crowned with its church and mill, or Writtle, which we know is slumbering in rural peace behind the skirting shrubberies to our left, was the Caesaromagus of the Roman conqueror, this green sward may have been pressed by hostile hoofs, and the hilltop may have gleamed with the watch-fires of the veterans who had over-run the world. The house was originally built about a century ago, by Sir John Comyns, Chief Baron of the Exchequer, but its character was entirely altered, its grounds tastefully laid out, and the park considerably extended by the late possessor, who purchased of C H Kortright, Esq.; and a book of drawings in the study by Mr Repton, shows the former and present appearance of the house and grounds. The hall is a noble apartment, enriched with several specimens of a sculpture and seagliola marble columns; and from this we pass to the drawing room - rather the drawing room and study combined - whose walls are thickly lined with the literary treasures of the ancients, of France, Italy, and England, in splendid bindings, while the rich rose-wood panelling of the doors, and the noble chimney mirror flinging back a duplicate of the interior, give the apartment an air of pleasing luxury, opening as it does to the south and south-west upon a conservatory, heated by water pipes, and in which the gay fuschia, running to the height of 12 or 16 feet, drops its blood-red flowers, or the more fragile natives of warmer climes spread forth their perfumed leaves and their gilded blossoms, forming altogether

"As sweet a bower
As e'er held Houri in the heathenish heaven".

The Dining, Billiard, Breakfast and Music rooms, which are noble, though not very spacious, are adorned with statues and busts, and a good few paintings, amongst which are a full length portrait of the late proprietor, and smaller portraits of his two sons and other members of the family. The bed-chambers are good, numbering, we believe, twenty-nine, many of them fenced from the northern blast of winter with double sashes; and every domestic apartment bears traces of thoughtful skill, which however we tarry not to describe, lest our passing sketch should dwindle into a formal catalogue.

The grounds and gardens, perhaps, more attract the attention of the visitor than the mansion itself. Sloping away towards Widford is an extended lawn, and beyond the velvet turf rise meadow and corn fields, village church, and town - a landscape on which is shown by nature's hand all the richness and variety of Essex scenery, for though we have no mountains capped with thunder clouds, or torrents rushing terrifically by, we have gentle hills topped with a busy hamlet of wavering crop, and which lightened up, as now, by a summer sun, look 'majestically gay'. To the right, adjacent to the London road, but sheltered from view by the spreading trees, is the extensive kitchen gardens in which the lengthened graperie teem with their ripe and ripening loads, and the peach, apricot, nectarine, fig and strawberry houses, with the melon ground send forth a luscious perfume, which makes the wanderer along the walks almost imagine himself

"In the land of cedar and vine,
Where the trees ever blossom, the beams ever shine;
Where the tints of the earth and the hue of the sky,
In colour though varied in beauty may vie".

While adjoining to these are Dutch pits, and all the inventions which mechanical and horticultural skill have matured for setting the seasons at defiance and loading the dining table with the delicacies of summer, even while old winter is lingering round our doors, and grumbling in the chimney-tops.

Crossing the lawn to the left, and passing through 'sheltered walks and alleys green', we arrive at a short tunnel, over which art has twisted the fantastic tops of old pollard trees with an air of rustic negligence; and on emerging from this a fine sheet of water, with the shrubberies, walks, and flower gardens, burst at once upon the view the beauties rendered more beautiful by the artificial gloom from which we have just escaped. Passing on through a wilderness of sweets, the whole laid out in the most perfect taste, we reach the extensive conservatory. To attempt an enumeration of even the principal floricultural varieties which here flourish in their warmed exotic beds, even when nature without is barren and bare and

> "The violet by the moss-grey stone
> Hath laid her weary head".

would extend our article to two or three decently sized volumes of botanical illustrations. The conservatory is nearly three hundred feet in length, the whole warmed by hot water flowing through pipes, and the walks paved with Portland stone, while without we are met on every side with the blossom and perfume of the more hardy plants of our own and other climes, the whole spreading around that pleasing voluptuous languor experienced by the summer evening loiterer beneath a more southern sky -

> "For dull the eye, the heart is dull
> That cannot feel how fair,
> Amid all beauty beautiful
> The tender blossoms are;
> How delicate the gauzy frill,
> How rich the branchy stem,
> How soft the voice when birds are still,
> And flowers sing hymns to them."

In the nooks and corners are little arbours, so thickly sheltered that a sunbeam can never penetrate them, the sides composed of moss, and the floors curiously laid with dead apples; and about the centre of this floral fairyland is the statuary-house, rich with various productions of the labouring chisel. Bronze statutes are also scattered about the grounds, and moated islands in miniature raise their heads, while a row of orange trees send forth at once the softening perfumes from the ripe fruit and the blossoms. Indeed art and taste have walked hand in hand through the domain, and rendered it all that wealth could reasonably sigh for or the English gentleman desire.

Even after death a good and faithful servant could be

remembered; behind the small church at Over Stowey a memorial leans against the ancient walls. It reads -

In memory of James Horsenell who lived 45 years in the service of P C Labouchere, Esq., of Hylands, Essex, and of his son Henry Labouchere, Lord Taunton. Died at Over Stowey on the 20th November 1870 in the 60th year of his age.

We only yield thee what is thine
Thy will be done.

Lady Taunton has placed this cross in memory of this long and faithful servant.

Dorothy Labouchere moved to Upper Grosvenor Street, London, and died there on 15th May, 1859, aged 89.

'Exhibition Extraordinary in the Horticultural Room' by George Cruikshank, 1 January, 1826. One of the characters portrayed is Pierre Caesar Labouchere

JOHN ATTWOOD [OWNER 1839-1858]

John Attwood was born in June, 1781, the eldest son of James and Phoebe Attwood of Halesowen. Little is known of his early life, but his mark on Essex society was to be significant.

John was a man of great enterprise and originality and had made a fortune from the founding and the eventual sale of the Corngreaves Iron Works, near Birmingham, and also the sale of the Corngreaves estate. He had ideas of grandeur and wished to be the founder of a great Essex family, which he hoped would be graced by a peerage.

In 1834 he was involved in the interminable lawsuit of *Small v. Attwood*, which resulted in John's favour. He was so delighted with his victory that he purchased the finest brougham and pair of horses that he could procure in London and presented them to Sir Thomas Wilde, his leading counsel, to whom he had already paid the enormous sum of six thousand guineas. The horses were named Small and Attwood. The case was so long and complicated that the total weight of the papers used weighed six tons!

It concerned the purchase, in 1825, of John's Corngreaves Estate, Dudley Wood, and other properties by John Taylor, James Henry Shears and Robert Small for the sum of £600,000. The lawsuit arose out of this purchase.

His first steps up the ladder of fame, for he already had the fortune, was the ownership of a large country estate - Hylands. In October, 1839, he purchased the 750 acres estate by private contract for £50,000 from the executors of P C Labouchere; he also bought Widford Hall at the same time. His next step was to become a Member of Parliament; this would enable him to steer through a private Act which would, by sheer coincidence, assist his project for a railway line from Harwich to Manningtree.

John stood as Conservative candidate for the Borough of Harwich on 30th June, 1841, and won the seat. However, three petitions were presented to Parliament against John and Major Beresford (Harwich at that time had two M.Ps) on the grounds of bribery to the sum of £10,000 and to treating and corruption. An agreement was reached before a Parliamentary Commission could sit and so, in 1842, Major Beresford was forced to retire. Sir Denis Le Marchant, who himself had spent £1,000 and yet had finished at the bottom of the poll, was allowed to stand unopposed by John and his agent: all the petitions were then withdrawn.

John, now secure in his country seat, was keen to have a mansion to meet his new position in society. He already had Holly Lodge at Harwich, but needed a much larger home to entertain. He therefore engaged a prominent architect and designer to plan new additions and redecoration of Hylands. The commission fell to the capable hands of John Buonarotti Papworth [1775-1847].

Between 1842 and 1845 John Attwood commissioned Papworth to prepare plans to remodel and extend the house. Papworth had considerable experience of carrying out alterations to existing houses, but, although his work to the interior of Hylands was to enhance the house, his extensions that were eventually to be built between 1847 and 1848 were to do little to improve its exterior appearance.

Plans in the Drawings Collection of the Royal Institute of British Architects shows Papworth's original intention was for the wings to remain un-altered, thus preserving the drawing room and conservatory, and for two new wings to be added on the north facing side of the house, connected to the existing bay windows and running at 450 to the main house. One of the new wings was to have contained a new dining room, an idea which must have been seriously considered, as a larger scale drawing of this wing also survives. The junction between the wings and the house was clumsy and would have done little to add to Hylands' elegance.

The plan was apparently rejected and a drastic remodelling of the interior was embarked upon; a contemporary account describes how the rooms were largely re-erected and the state rooms were fitted out with almost reckless luxury. By 1848, a year after Papworth's death, Attwood was to have completed his work and Hylands was remodelled out of all recognition.

Structural iron was installed into floors and roofs and the semi-circular bays at the rear were splayed to strengthen them for their extension upwards.

The Repton designed drawing room and conservatory were demolished to basement level, leaving only the partial shell of the wing, into which Papworth inserted a drawing room 36ft 8in by 23ft 2in and a library 36ft 8in by 22ft 6in, both approached from a salon. The semi-circular bay window was also to disappear from this wing and, when it was rebuilt, a new rectangular canopy was added to the outside of the house.

Part of the west wing was gutted to form the banqueting hall. The decoration of this room is an elaborate essay in Victorian Baroque and is in marked contrast to the rooms in the east wing. Were it not for detailed descriptions of the room in the sales catalogue for 1854, it would be easy to ascribe its decoration to a later date. The decoration of the drawing room is equally fine, but more typical of the period. Both the east and west wings were to have an extra storey added.

In the centre block the breakfast room was to be shortened and an open Ionic screen demolished, so allowing a passageway directly from the kitchens and into the new dining room. The original Georgian staircase was taken out and, having combined the hallway with an existing room, it was formed into a large grand staircase. Only the hallway was to escape the destruction of the neo-classical interiors.

On the first floor further rooms were added; there were now ladies' boudoirs; two state bedrooms with dressing rooms, bathroom and water closet; seven other bedrooms; four dressing rooms and bathrooms; seven secondary bedrooms; three large store-rooms fitted with hot air pipes capable for use as drying closets; and four large apartments for servants, with store rooms, water closets, etc. On the second floor was built nine superior bedrooms and nurseries.

The portico was brought down and replaced with a wider and deeper *port cochère* with an Ionic tetra-style front. The hipped and dormered attic storey was removed and a further storey was added, having a high parapet, adding even more bedrooms and nurseries with spectacular views over the park.

New two storey domestic offices were built to replace those demolished: a kitchen 35ft 6in by 24ft, housekeeper's room, two still rooms, head butler's apartment with fire proof plate room, steward's room, servants' hall, French cook's offices, scullery, game and meat larder that was fitted with marble dressers and stands, a washing room, ironing room with hot closet, mangle room contiguous to the drying yard, clothes room, lamp room, and minor offices, partially attached, but approached from the kitchen by a covered way, an extensive dairy fitted with marble dressers with washing room attached; within a short distance was a bake house and a brew house.

The relief that is now to be seen on the east wing of Hylands is a patent stone relief made of Coade stone. This material is weather-proof and frost-resistant, which was a great improvement in earlier attempts for an artificial stone. The panel is set in the terrace wall of Attwood's new wing, depicting the Roman corn goddess, Ceres, reclining on the ground in a classical pose. She was also identified in antiquity with the Greek corn goddess, Demeter, who governed the fruits of the earth, also shown in the composition. It was probably the work of John Bacon the Elder, RA [1740-1799].

The mould was probably made some time between 1769 and 1777 and this mould was continually reused until the end of the factory. It cannot therefore be dated accurately and may have been bought by a previous owner to adorn some part of a gardening structure and subsequently moved or it may have been purchased by Papworth or John Attwood at the closing down sale of Coade artifacts held on 21st July, 1843: it is known that Papworth used Coade stone on other commissions.

In both the 1841 and the 1851 Censuses John Attwood seems not to have been present at his Hylands estate, only staff were present, they are:

1841 Census	Name	Age	Occupation
Hylands House	Elizabeth Parkin	28	Servant
	Jane Smith	24	Servant
	Hannah Wix	22	Servant
	John Burton	32	Man Servant
Hylands Bath House	Joseph Newcourt	60	Carpenter
	Sarah Newcourt	65	

1851 Census	Age	Occupation	Place of Birth
Charles Kennedy	40	Gardener	Scotland
Harriah Warmington	30	House keeper	Shrewsbury
Robert Raven	40	Servant	Rettendon, Essex
Sarah Raven	30	Servant	Birch, Essex
William Smith	19	House Servant	Chelmsford

As John looked across his domain he found that all was not as he wished. He could see in the distance the tops of other properties above the sky line. Therefore Mill Green House, Coptfold Hall and many smaller farms and properties were purchased and then demolished. There seems to have been some argument in the family, probably over the money he was spending - some £200,000 in all. Whatever the troubles were, the end result was the same. Bricks from Coptfold Hall were sold to the Eastern Counties Railway and were used in the construction of the Seven Arches Bridge at Brentwood.

Not only was no one else's property to be seen, but the general traffic on the public highway was also to be kept at a distance. In 1841 John paid £1,000 to the parishes of Writtle, Chelmsford and Margaretting for the privilege of closing several public roads that ran through his estate. They were then blocked off and trees planted at the crossroads to bar the traffic of lesser mortals from crossing his lands. The whole estate now consisted of 4,300 acres stretching from the Chignals to Margaretting, with a massive, lofty brick wall, nearly a mile long, screening the house from the London road.

This activity was not without some benefit to the local inhabitants. The money given to the parish of Writtle was used to provide clothing, bread and fuel for the poor and, later, in 1843, a school, now demolished. was built behind the church at Widford, its foundation stone carrying John's name.

However, John's political career was not proceeding to plan. In the following General Election in July/August, 1847, at which John was elected as Liberal-Conservative M.P., further allegations were made against him. A Parliamentary Enquiry was set up to investigate the complaints which were, amongst other corrupt practices, that sailing vessels giving free rides to voters of his opponent were supposed to sail inside the harbour wall, but were accidentally diverted out to sea and, with wind and tide against them, were not able to dock until after the polling stations had closed!

The Committee reported to the House of Commons in 1848 that -

John Attwood, Esq., is not duly elected to serve as Burgess in the present Parliament for the Borough of Harwich.

That the said John Attwood, Esq., was, by his agents, guilty of bribery.

That the last election for the Borough of Harwich was, so far as regards the return of the said John Attwood, Esq., a void election.

A new election was held in March, 1848, at Harwich. But the loss of his parliamentary seat was just the start of John's financial troubles. The extravagance of changes and extensions to all his many properties was a financial strain and his speculations on the Stock Exchange were beginning to go wrong; soon all the estate was mortgaged to various people, the total being somewhere in the region of £175,000.

On 17th November, 1850, he sold sold Shenfields and Killigrews Farms to Mr John Philpott. but his fall was rapid, as creditors became more insistent. At a meeting of his creditors in February, 1855, it was announced that he was in debt to the tune of £300,000, his downfall being due to his speculation in the price of pig-iron.

In March, 1854, Hylands had been placed on the open market in one lot - a total of over 4,289 acres, of which the park itself was 590 acres, but there were no buyers.

The sale catalogue gives a more detailed list of the many buildings. The conservatory of 250ft in the pleasure gardens, the kitchen gardens, four pineries, two peach houses and the attached gardener's cottage with fruit rooms, onion chambers, potting sheds and mushroom house. Homestead Farm consisted of a barn, stable, cow house, cowshed, piggeries, hayhouse, sheds, cart lodge and slaughter house.

The stable block consisted of five stables accommodating eighteen horses, six large carriage houses, harness and corn rooms, a long range of hay lofts and two cart sheds. Attached was a residence for the head coachman, with a carpenter's shop and offices.

John had added to the park large expanses of land and, though of no special interest, it is still possible to trace the route of several roads and one can walk many hundreds of yards between the lines of ancient hawthorn trees, whose branches form a perfect tunnel.

On 6th June, 1854, Hylands was again put up for sale in seventy-three lots; no purchaser was found and the sale was to drag on. The furniture was sold by auction between 22nd and 31st August.

John left the country and died, quite unnoticed, at Boulogne-sur-Mer in France in 1865. Agents administered the estate until it was eventually split into seventy lots to be sold separately.

This was to happen to other properties Attwood owned at Harwich, in London and places all around this country, and even as far as America.

Hylands was to enter a period of four years in limbo. In 1855 the administrators sold some oak trees in the park, which were due to be felled by Sadd's, the timber merchants, but an objector made an injunction through the courts and the deal was not allowed to take place.

Engraving of Hylands House from the Sale Catalogue, 1854

Chelmsford Library

ARTHUR PRYOR [OWNER 1858-1904]

Arthur Pryor was born on 7th January, 1816, at Baldock, Hertfordshire, the third son of Vickris and Jane Pryor, and entered Eton College in 1829. Here he founded the Sixpenny Cricket Club, where for a sixpence any student could belong to the club and would thus be ineligible for 'fagging'.

After Oxford University, where he earned his Bachelor of Arts, he became a partner in the brewing firm of Truman, Hanbury, Buxton & Co in London in 1839, thus maintaining a strong family link with the brewery. All the partners in the firm had to prove their worth and, in the partners' book, it was noted that it was 'agreed to inform Mr Arthur Pryor that we accept him as a partner, according to the articles. We shall expect him to work diligently and if he does so, as we trust he will, we shall, after sufficient time for probation admit him as a working partner'.

Arthur was a great sportsman and was to become renowned for his fishing, shooting and other activities. In 1838 he joined the Marylebone Cricket Club and on his death was the oldest member on the roll.

In 1841 he married Elizabeth Sophia Dew and was to have four sons and five daughters. With such a big family a large house was needed and so Arthur started negotiations for the purchase of Hylands in 1857. He finally bought 843 acres of the estate in January, 1858, for the sum of £45,000 and moved into the house in that November, from their previous residence, Dover House, Roehampton.

The redecoration of several rooms took place, the reception room in the east wing received treatment: a copy of the *Daily Telegraph* dated 29th November, 1858, was found packed behind a marble mantelpiece that was moved in 1987. In the Banqueting room an inscription above the cornice of the coved ceiling has also been found, reading

G Lothian
R Thompson   Painters Feby 12th 1859   J Lommas, Foreman
W Young

On 5th April, 1859, Arthur became a Justice of the Peace

and Deputy Lieutenant of the county and served as High Sheriff of Essex for 1866/7. His only excursion into party politics was to become Chairman of the Mid-Essex Conservative Association. He had a new mixed parochial school for a hundred children built behind the church at Widford and was, later, in 1894, to enlarge it.

The Crimean War had shown that the British Army was in a poor state, and as a result was undergoing large-scale changes. In 1859 and 1860 there were manoeuvres at Hylands. That of 1860 was reported in the *Times*:

"A review and sham fight is to take place at Hylands on Saturday, 4th August, 1860. Besides three troops of Essex Yeomanry, there will be in the field a body of Uxbridge Yeomanry and companies of Essex Volunteers, the whole battalion of the county being invited. The Honourable Artillery Company, the Victoria Rifles, the Tower Hamlets Company, and Messrs Truman, Hanbury & Company's Corps. Altogether it is expected two to three thousand volunteers of various corps will attend."

By now Hylands was a large and busy environment engaged in the function of serving a large family. To gauge how many servants it took to run such an undertaking can be easily gained from the Census returns, such as that of 1861:

Name of Occupier	Age	Status	Place of birth
Pryor, Arthur	45	Head	Hertfordshire
Pryor, Elizabeth Sophia	46	Wife	Devonshire
Pryor, Lucy Elizabeth	16	Daughter	Surrey, Wandsworth
Pryor, Arthur Vickris	14	Son	Surrey, Wandsworth
Pryor, Edith Lucy	13	Daughter	Surrey, Wandsworth
Pryor, Emily	11	Daughter	Norfolk, Hunstanton
Pryor, Edward	10	Son	Norfolk,Castle Rises
Pryor, Robert	8	Son	Surrey, Roehampton
Pryor, Roderick	6	Son	Surrey, Roehampton
Pryor, Katherine	4	Daughter	Surrey, Roehampton
St Aubyn, Eliza	42	Visitor	Leyton
Worthington, [illegible]	30	Visitor	Middlesex, London
Ayres, Henry	36	Butler	Bucks, Ovring
Smith, George	25	Footman	Gloucs, Leamington
Bull, William	18	Footman	Middlesex, London
Wasteman, Edward	23	Groom	Herts,Bishops Stortford
Thomson, Henry	26	Undergardener	Scotland
Mendmer, William	23	Undergardener	Herefordshire

Rich, Elizabeth	41	Housekeeper	Somerset, Stoke
Firth, Maria	30	Lady's maid	Yorks, Wakefield
Cudmore, Eliza	33	Laundrymaid	Suffolk, Bury St Edmunds
Pratchett, Susan	18	Laundrymaid	Herts, Hatfield
Buckley, Charlotte	32	Housemaid	Ireland
Saunders, Elizabeth	28	Housemaid	Essex, Chelmsford
Waters, Eliza	25	Nurse	Surrey, Reigate
Walpole, Sophes	21	Nurse	Norfolk, Northrepps
Cox, Maria	29	Kitchenmaid	Essex, Hanningfield
Story, Jane	16	Scullerymaid	Cornwall
Read, Mahalah	48	Housemaid	Surrey, Egham

Arthur purchased the living of Widford and, with this, he became responsible for the appointment of the local parson. Arthur and his wife, who was a deeply religious woman, were brought more closely into touch with church affairs. But the structure of the local church was in a dilapidated state and, for Arthur, not large or grand enough and so he was to finance its demolition in 1861 at a cost of £4,000. On Saturday, 15th June, 1861, the foundation stone for the new church was laid and the building of St Mary's was completed to the design of James Piers St Aubyn [1815-1895] of London at a cost of £4-5,000. It is interesting that St Aubyn's wife, Eliza, was visiting Hylands in 1861 and was thus listed in the Census return. The opening service for the new church was held on 22nd July, 1862. A new set of bells was hung and two of these bear the inscription 'The gift of Arthur Pryor of Hylands'.

Arthur's daughters were to become associated with Widford church and, between 1862 and 1872, Lucy Elizabeth, Emily and Katherine were to hold the position of organist. Arthur himself was to be churchwarden from 1863 until 1904.

On the Christmas Eve of 1861 a shoot was held on the estate and many birds fell to Arthur's gun. A local hunting journal reported that Arthur, who was known as an excellent shot, with four other guns, killed 25 brace of partridge.

In 1867, he became, like Sir John Comyns, a Governor of King Edward Grammar School in Chelmsford.

The Census return of 1871 lists -

An early photograph portrait of Arthur Pryor

An undated photograph of the servants at Hylands

Name	Age	Profession	Place of Birth
Arthur Pryor	56	Brewer	Baldock, Herts.
Elizabeth Sophia Pryor	57		Star Cross, Devon
Edith Louisa Pryor	23		Wandsworth, Surrey
Emily Pryor	21		Hunstanton, Norfolk
Edmund Pryor	20	Merchant Clerk	Castle Rising, Norfolk
Robert Pryor	18	Scholar	Roehampton, Surrey
Roderick Pryor	16	Scholar	Roehampton, Surrey
Katherine Pryor	13	Scholar	Roehampton, Surrey
Henrietta Restall	50	Governess	Marylebone, London
James Adcock	45	Butler	Ticknall, Derbyshire
William Brise	28	Footman	Lt Bowne, Herts.
Jesse Head	22	Footman	Eynsford, Herts.
Thomas Halsey	21	Groom	Rushden, Herts.
Joseph Perry	19	Stablehelper	Roxwell, Essex
James Grout	18	Stablehelper	Steven, Essex
Richard Abbott	21	Houseman	E. Bergholt, Suffolk
Barbara Hannah	44	Domestic Housekeeper	Wigtown, Scotland
Louisa Johnson	27	Lady'smaid	Merton, Middx.
Elsa Ford	23	Lady'smaid	Staines, Middx.
Ruth Haskins	27	Cook	Swansea
Ellen Bolton	21	Kitchenmaid	Shalestone, Bucks.
Emily Wellacott	19	Scullerymaid	Sandford, Exeter
Jessie Hardy	19	Dairymaid	Brenckham, Inverness
Adeline Peacock	16	Schoolroom maid	Widford, Essex
Elizabeth Byers	29	Housemaid	Halifax, Nova Scotia
Elizabeth Southgate	23	Domestic Housemaid	Fingringhoe, Essex
Caroline Wensley	24	Domestic Housemaid	Bury, Devon
Anna Maria Lewis	22	Laundrymaid	Chelmsford, Essex
Eliza Cox	24	Laundrymaid	Middleton, Norfolk
Elizabeth Quin	19	Laundrymaid	Writtle, Essex

Widford was not the only church to benefit from his patronage. Mrs Pryor noticed that the spiritual needs of Galleywood were inadequately served by a chapel of ease in the church school at The Eagle crossroads and suggested that a scheme be put in hand for a church on Galleywood Common. The architect called upon was again James Piers St Aubyn.

18th June, 1872, was to be a day of double celebration for the Pryor family. In the morning Emily was married to Walter Edward Grimston at Widford church and in the afternoon the foundation stone for St Michael and All Angels, Galleywood, was laid: the building is unique as it is the only church in the country to have been built within a horse racing circuit.

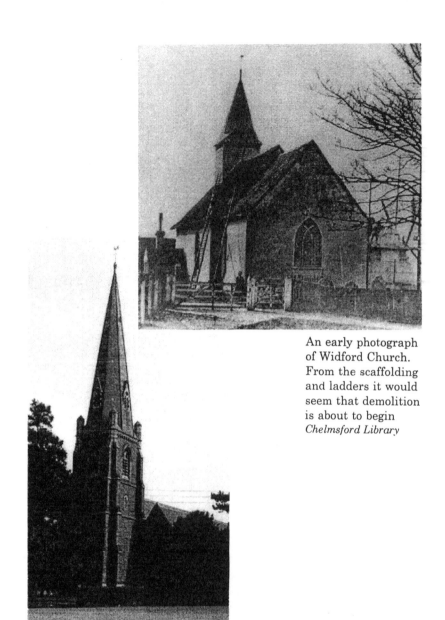

An early photograph
of Widford Church.
From the scaffolding
and ladders it would
seem that demolition
is about to begin
Chelmsford Library

Galleywood Church

Arthur, although financing the construction of this church, was only on one occasion able to set foot inside the edifice to worship. This was because a visiting clergyman had, on the first Sunday before the appointed incumbent had taken up his duties, given a sermon mildly in favour of purgatory: this so horrified Arthur that he could never again be persuaded to attend another service in the church on which he had spent over £6,000.

This was not to prevent the celebration of the consecration of the church on 29th September, 1873, and the Pryors were among the 750 people present.

The *Essex Chronicle* reported that:

On Monday was consummated a noble and generous work which was commenced in June of last year, when Mr Pryor, of Hylands, laid the foundation stone of a new church on Galleywood common, a memorial of his generosity which now stands out as one of the most prominent objects in the landscape for many miles of Chelmsford. The fabric and fittings having been completed, the ceremony of consecration was performed on Monday by the Lord Bishop of the Diocese, amid every appropriate demonstration of heartiness and enthusiasm. The church is a handsome structure and the fact that Mr Pryor has not only presented it to the newly formed parish of Galleywood, but endorsed it with a good living, is an additional proof of his liberty and his attachment to our mother church.

The day of consecration will be doubly marked by the poor of the parish, all of whom were treated by Mrs Pryor to a substantial dinner in the school after the opening ceremony. Mr Brown of the Eagle Inn was also commissioned to feast the bell ringers, 14 in number, after their arduous labours, and it is proper to record here that on Saturday afternoon the men who had been engaged on the building were served with a capital dinner (ordered by Mrs Pryor) at the Blue Lion Inn, and Mr Neale, clerk of the works, presided; Mr Bowers, foreman over the masons, being in the vice chair. The health of Mr and Mrs Pryor was drunk with much enthusiasm and, among the other toasts, were the health of the architect and builders, and the health of the host and hostess.

The builders of the church were Messrs. Putnam and Fotheringham of London, who completed the building in the remarkable space of 364 days! A band of change ringers from Benington, Hertfordshire, where Arthur's second cousin, John

Earle Pryor, was rector, came especially for the service and rang 5,060 changes.

Though Arthur was a keen fisherman, he also made great efforts in the conservation of wildlife. He preserved game strictly on all his farms. He tried unsuccessfully to introduce trout to the stream running through the park.

Throughout the 19th century the gardeners looked after the park with pride and, each year, a pilgrimage was made to the Royal Horticultural Society's Annual Show, medals being won for a number of exhibits. Fêtes, band concerts and all manner of social activities were held at Hylands. In 1873 Arthur was the host to the Chelmsford Horticultural Society's annual show.

Three lodges were built: Widford Lodge, built of brick, stucco and tiled, was one storey high, containing three rooms with outer offices and garden; London Lodge, built of ornamental brick stucco and thatched, was one storey high, with a porch, having four rooms with outer offices and garden; and Margaretting Lodge was built of brick and slate, with four rooms, plus outer offices and garden.

The walls that had surrounded the vegetable and flower gardens to the north of the house were demolished and Mr Bowman soon occupied a gardener's bungalow built of brick and slate.

The *Gardeners' Chronicle* of 11th June, 1881, gives a vivid description of the pleasure gardens that were the responsibility of Mr Bowman. His residence, demolished in 1975, had an extensive view of the park and its front was covered with mysotis, wallflowers, silene and spring bedding plants.

In the flower garden some one thousand Belvoir Castle and Tom Thumb wallflowers were planted, also two thousand *Mysotis Dissitiflora*, daisies in great number including white and red, *Aubretia Purpurea*, large beds of yellow violas and Cliveden purple pansies, with masses of *Pilene Pendula Compacta*. Bougainvillaea was grown to perfection, also *Lapageria Alba*, gloxinias, calceolarias and pelargoniums.

In the kitchen garden, which was of 8 acres, there were 16 houses devoted to fruit growing, 4 vineries and 2 small vineries, a house for French beans also contained a Osborn's Prolific fig in pots, 3 peach house, 2 pineries, 2 melon houses, 2 houses for strawberries, as well as pyramidal pear trees and sea kale grown extensively. Across the park was an apple orchard of four to five acres.

In 1876 the clerks at Truman's presented Arthur with a portrait of himself. In a charming letter to him they said that, "We also look forward to distant generations of Partners and Clerks". Also surviving is a letter from Henry Villebois apologising for his absence at the ceremony, "Unfortunately, I have to entertain Royalty the whole of that week, only regretting that, as it interferes with my being with you".

The renewed taxation on beer and the restricting licensing laws, brought in under William Ewart Gladstone, increased the financial problems of the brewing industry and so Arthur led the battle of over 700 breweries to get another tax on brewers' licenses repealed - but without success.

When it came to railways Arthur had a totally different view to that of Pierre Labouchere. Whereas it was a curse to Pierre, Arthur utilised the proximity of the line to its full advantage. In 1881 Arthur approached the Great Eastern about the possibility of a railway siding being constructed and, having signed an agreement on 5th January, 1882, the siding was built and still exists just off Private Road, Galleywood. It runs parallel to the main Chelmsford-London line and British Rail still use it occasionally.

Arthur used the little railway halt to bring his guests from London in a railway carriage that would be shunted on to the siding and then his guests could disembark to waiting carriage and horses to be brought to the house. As well as social uses, the commercial possibilities were likewise used. Fuel was brought in for the expanding brickworks at Galleywood, while vegetables and fruit were transported to London's expanding and ever demanding public need.

Arthur was a keen supporter of the Chelmsford and Essex Hospital and laid its foundation stone in 1882.

Truman's were to become a limited liability company in 1888 and Arthur was to play an important rôle in its success.

Eventually his position in the firm changed from senior partner to Chairman of the Board and the period from the changeover until his retirement in 1897 was characterised by an increasingly scientific approach to the age old art of brewing.

Although Arthur could no longer shoot over the once vast estate of Attwood's day, he gradually increased the size of the estate by buying up nearby properties, whenever they came up for sale, such as Widford Hall from Mr G C King in 1859 and Robjohn's Farm in 1888. At some time in the 1880s Arthur had a fainting spell and had to give up following the hounds.

By 1891 the census shows that the elder children had left home and it seems that young visitors were staying at the time of the census:

Name	Relation to Head of House	Age	Occupation	Place of Birth
Arthur Prior		75	Brewer	Baldock, Herts.
Elizabeth Sophia Pryor	Wife	76		Burleigh, Devon
Guy Francis Pryor	Grandson	14		Camberwell, Surrey
Katherine Pryor	Granddaughter	11	Scholar	Montague Sq., London
Elizabeth Horatia Pryor		9	Scholar	Montague Sq., London
John Arthur Pryor		7	Scholar	Writtle, Essex
Mary Noel Grimston		10	Scholar	London
Eleanor Vera Grimston		7	Scholar	London
Sydney Lewis		29	Domestic Butler	Alfrick, Worcs.
Catherine Day		44	Housekeeper	Gt. Burton, Peeledies
Mary Frances Maggs		38	Lady'smaid	White Parish, Wilts.
Annise Lupton		54	Cook	Ambleside, Westmoreland
Maggie Jane Campbell		27	Laundrymaid	Kirkcudbright
Annie Davis		29	Housekeeper	Turnsuade, Aberdeen
Annie Wheaton		23	Laundrymaid	Landston, Camb.
Beatrice Simmonds		24	Kitchenmaid	Harrow on the Hill
Mary Hester Hawker		20	Schoolroom maid	St Johns Wood, London
Olive Heron		20	Dairymaid	Lancashire
Lucy Blanks		19	Laundrymaid	Writtle, Essex
Ellen Burden		24	Housemaid	Oxford
Winifred Stracey		16	Scullerymaid	Pyrford, Surrey
Annie Hiron		19	Housemaid	Posborne, Derbyshire
George Gooch		19	Footman	Norfolk
Harry Ranson		24	Hallman	Ipswich, Suffolk
Elsie Cardiant		24	Young Lady'smaid	Lambeth, Surrey

In 1897 he fell ill and for the following years was unable to pursue his love of fishing and shooting.

'Squire Pryor', as he was sometimes called, had, for nearly thirty years, rented an extensive grouse moor in Inverness-shire. He was also proud of his achievements as a salmon fisherman, having had the good fortune to land the largest salmon taken with fly and rod, up to that time. The fish weighed 57 pounds and, after being set up, it found a home in the Duke of Roxborough's castle, whilst an oil painting of it hung in the hall at Hylands for many years.

The agricultural depression of the late 19th century was a source of concern to Arthur and he sent a succession of letters to the *Times* on the subject, causing quite a controversy. So it was not surprising that, when in 1898 a great storm struck southern England, he refunded a half year's rent to all his tenants whose crops had been badly affected. The well-being of his tenants was of great concern to Arthur, especially this with a low income. He was a great admirer of the Post Office Savings Bank and urged people to use it. He even purchased space in the local newspapers for them to carry details of this new banking service. In celebration of Queen Victoria's Jubilee in 1897, Arthur offered to entertain the people of Widford to a dinner or send them to London, fare pre-paid, with 2/6d to spend.

Arthur was a tall and stately figure and throughout his life his handsome figure could be easily identified by the style of dress that was uniquely his own: a large collar, a large bow and a tall black silk hat.

His beloved wife, Elizabeth, died at 5 o'clock on Saturday evening, 8th October, 1898, of an apoplexy. She had been a source of strength to him and to all local folk. It was not unusual for her to stay all day at the bedside of some sick local woman, who could not pay for a nurse. Elizabeth even provided pupils at Widford Sunday School with a proper outfit, the girls with hats and cloaks and the boys with hats.

Arthur was to continue his life without Elizabeth, but his health was gradually deteriorating and he was to become an invalid for the last seven years of his life. He suffered an attack of pruritus in July, 1904, and he took to his bed some three weeks before his eventual death. He had suffered a slight stroke on 18th September and died peacefully at 10.45 in the evening of 25th September, 1904, aged eighty-eight. At his death he was the longest living Old Etonian.

Arthur's funeral service was held on 29th September and, according to his wishes, his body was carried from Hylands to Widford in one of the farm wagons. Arthur and Elizabeth were laid together in the surrounds of Widford church.

Since one of Arthur's attributes was a strong sense of humour, perhaps he would have appreciated the rather irreverent attitude of some of his young descendants, who referred to his making sure of a place in Heaven by building the churches of Widford and Galleywood as 'Grandfather's fire insurance'.

Arthur Vickris Pryor, his eldest son, succeeded him. He already had his home at Melton Mowbray and decided not to live permanently at Hylands. But he maintained the place for some time and became Widford's churchwarden. Then he decided to rent out Hylands and a suitable lease was needed.

Widford church was to be endowed with two stained glass windows: the first window of the nave reads 'In memory of Elizabeth Sophia Pryor, wife of Arthur Pryor, who died Oct 8th 1898' and shows Martha, Elizabeth and Mary; the west window of the north aisle reads 'In memory of Arthur Pryor of Hylands who rebuilt the church. Died Sept 25th 1904.' and shows Faith, Hope and Charity. This window was dedicated by Dr Johnson, Suffragan Bishop and Archdeacon of Colchester on Sunday, 7th January, 1906.

A full-length portrait of Arthur Pryor hangs in the Boardroom of Truman, Hanbury & Buxton's offices in Brick Lane, London.

SIR DANIEL FULTHORPE GOOCH [OWNER 1908-1920]

The Gooch family originated from Beccles, Suffolk. The new owner of Hylands was descended from a family of engineers closely associated with the Great Western Railway, both Daniel's father and grandfather being pioneers of steam.

Daniel was born on 25th May, 1869, the eldest son of Sir Henry Daniel and Lady Mary Gooch, and was educated at Trinity Hall, Cambridge. At some point in his life he gained the nickname 'Curly'. He became a Justice of the Peace in Berkshire and, on 23rd June, 1896, married May Winifred Monro of Clewer Hill: on the death of his father on 24th June, 1897, Daniel succeeded as the 3rd Baronet.

About 1906 Sir Daniel took up the lease of the Hylands estate and was so pleased with his new residence that he was to purchase the estate from Arthur Vickris Pryor the next year.

In December, 1907, Daniel engaged Frederick Chancellor & Son, architects, to prepare plans of improvements and alterations, including a new arched side entrance and an oak secondary staircase in the west wing. The banqueting room in the west wing was renovated and on a cedar board that was part of a covered damask wall panel an inscription was found. It reads, "Covered by F Porter c/o Wenley & Son, Chelmsford. 24/12/08."

Sir Daniel bought several nearby estates, including Child's Farm and Philip's Farm from Mr George Edison, Jordan's Farm from Mr James Eve and the Killigrew's estate in 1908.

On 16th December, 1908, Lady Gooch opened the new village hall at Writtle, half of its cost being borne by the Attwood Fund (founded by John Attwood). An earlier suggestion for the money had been for a library and institute building, but instead the village hall was constructed of red brick and could easily seat 300 people; it was to be named the Attwood Village Hall.

The late Harold Fairbank, OBE, was a student at the County Institute at Rainsford End Gardens, Chelmsford, and, as part of the horticultural course, he was to work at Hylands

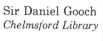

Sir Daniel Gooch
Chelmsford Library

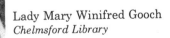

Lady Mary Winifred Gooch
Chelmsford Library

for three years shortly after the turn of the century. His father made arrangements with Mr Wilkinson, the gardener at Hylands, for young Harold to work there between terms. Cycling to work three miles each morning and working from 8 a.m. to 5.30 p.m. (4 on Saturdays), he received no pay or pocket money. He vividly recalled that his first job was to remove all the dead flowers off the rhododendrons: it was a task that was to take him two weeks! The foreman was eventually to take him off the job and sent him to work in the glasshouses.

There were between 16 and 20 gardeners and all would be utilised each day, as Sir Daniel and Lady Gooch entertained a great deal. Large shooting parties gathered at Hylands every Saturday during the season and so large amounts of flowers, fruit and vegetables were required by the domestic staff. It was rare to find less than twenty people were seated for lunch or dinner.

The large greenhouse in the middle of the pleasure garden consisted of a large palm house, a tropical house or 'stove' and a temperate house. William 'Billy' Heath, who was later to become Head Gardener at Hylands, grew Malmaison carnations: his expertise in growing them was to be passed on to Harold. The name of W Heath and Son was advertised as supplying dianthus plants. A special day came when Harold was to accompany the head gardener to an exhibition at the Royal Horticultural Society's Hall in Vincent Square, Westminster: they won a silver gilt medal.

Harold enjoyed his work there so much that he had himself taken on the permanent staff, instead of returning to college and did not sit his examinations, thus not qualifying for a further twenty years. After a few years, he did leave to broaden his experience elsewhere.

Sir Robert Gooch, Daniel's eldest son, remembers many of the staff and the considerable amount of work that was needed to manage such a large house; ten housemaids, a butler, a foot-man, several parlourmaids, fourteen garden staff, two chauffeurs, two cooks, three kitchen maids, a groom, an estate engineer, an estate agent and three gamekeepers. All the staff were used on the big occasions that were held at Hylands. One such event must have been on Saturday, 24th June, 1911, when a Coronation Fête was held by the Goochs, to which some 700 guests, mainly parishioners of Widford and the farm and cottage tenants of the estate and their children, were invited. The gardens were open to all and the Duke of Cornwall's Light Infantry Band from Gravesend played in the flower gardens. Coronation medals were distributed and games and sports were held to keep the children amused. In the marquee tea was served, with strawberries and cream, and on this very pleasant sunny day the gentlemen and their ladies could stroll around the grounds.

Galleywood school was in need of substantial repairs by 1912 and Sir Daniel and Lady Gooch were to meet the deficit of £30 from the £175 that was needed. Between 1908 and 1914 Sir Daniel was churchwarden for Widford church.

The Chelmsford Golf Club had been founded in 1893, with a nine hole course at Galleywood Common, but in 1910 he offered the the club a lease of some land for 21 years for anew course. This was built by James Macdonald of Harpenden for £750 and sat astride the main railway line at Widford. Its official opening was on 22nd June, 1911. Sir Daniel was to enjoy the proximity of this new sports facility and became President of the club from 1911 to 1913 and Captain from 1915 to 1920.

On 26th June, 1912, there was a society wedding at Hylands, making national, as well as local, news. The bride was Miss Dorothy Taylor from New York. With her parents she was a guest of Sir Daniel and Lady May prior to the ceremony and the reception was held at Hylands. This was no ordinary wedding!

The bridegroom was Mr Claude Grahame-White [1879-1959], the well-known aviator. The event became known as Britain's first aero-wedding and was the prelude to a barnstorming tour to rouse the nation to the increasing importance of the aeroplane. An aero-wedding would cause quite a stir today, but, at a time when few people had even seen an aircraft, it was hardly surprising that a very large crowd turned out to watch the proceedings.

The day before the ceremony there was a grand fête in the grounds of Hylands (no doubt more work for the ground staff!) and the prospective bridegroom was to give demonstration flights, but unfortunately he was delayed by some previous damage to his aeroplane. He eventually appeared over Hylands in the evening and, carefully avoiding the many trees, landed on the lawn. The wedding day dawned fine and sunny, to the delight of the social journalists and visiting aviators, as well as the families. A great gathering of the finest pilots in Europe attended and at time the noise of Grahame-White's friends' engines drowned the sound of Widford church's organ: the emerging couple were showered with confetti by one of the aeronauts.

The *Aeroplane* magazine included a poem on the aviator's wedding in its 27th June, 1912, issue

The Aviator's Wedding

A Congratulatory Ode

Dedicated to Mr and Mrs Claude Grahame-White

On wings of fancy lightly borne
we hailed the happy wedding morn
when our best pilot, Grahame-White,
Essayed his matrimonial flight.
His vast 'Cathedral', dim and grey,
was lent by Cody for the day,
The organ, blown by Stanley Lewin,
was deftly played by Mr Ewen;
While Mr Wakefield led the show,
for he's a vicar, as you know.
Robert Loraine, as well he can,
acted as Grahame-White's best man;
And once he gave a hollow groan,
because he thought the ring had flown.
The bride, in airy fabrics clad,
a sheaf of Arum lilies had.
Young Robinson, 'The Nation's Gift',
with Marcel did her train uplift.
The bridegroom wore most stylish clothes
(On strike his Taylor never goes!)
the bridesmaids put on airs, 'tis true,

71

in motor veils of pale sky-blue.
Sweet arias the choir then sang
and all the bells of Hendon rang.
Congratulations, quite a host
came early, by aerial Post.
Off with the films flew Mr Hucks
to Cheltenham Cinema de Luxe.
The guests dropped in from the sky,
For though they flew, they scorned a fly.
Some crossed the sea, Some flew from town,
and some from Bath had just Combe Down.
In a huge hanger, in the shade,
the costly wedding gifts were laid;
with, as detective at the door,
our trusted friend McCullum Mohr.
Brave Beaumont gave 'My Three Great Flights',
Mckenna sent some army kites;
A cigarette case, aptly chased,
was Latham's gift, in perfect taste.
Vedrines and Garros sent together
a trophy of an eagle's feather.
A fine stuffed heron in a case
from Orehousey held an honoured place.
From Mrs C de Beauvoir Stocks
two pairs of fleecy knitted socks.
A chest arrived from Zee Yee Lee,
containing pure celestial tea.
From Oscar Gnossipeliu
a cast of 'Peg', the Flying 'oss;
While in the area were seen
Skye terriers, from Frank Mclean.
An heirloom came from far away,
from Brindejonc des Moulinais.
The Women's Aerial League presented
a can of petrol sweetly scented.
Babe 'Jumbo' gave a trunk, brand new
He sent the bride a 'Mirror' too.
And Mr Adams, fond of jokes,
sent apples from his 'Hill of Oaks'.
While Salmet vowed on tour to take
to all kind friends some wedding cake.
Now Vol au Vent around was passed,

and potted larks were swallowed fast;
With wedding cake from Buszard's rare,
and also 'trifles, light as air'.
A lordly brace of flying fish
came steaming in a silver dish.
Bechamel sauce was present, too,
and champagne corks most gaily flew.
Requested by the genial host,
Commander Samson gave a toast
in which he firmly did declare
that Britain's strength lies in her 'air.
He hoped the bridegroom and the bride
all Wright through life would safely glide;
Together soar to heights of bliss,
and every cloud of trouble miss.
Then came farewell; too slow the train,
So off they went by aeroplane.
Odd shoes and rice, most neatly blended,
From Beatties biplane swift descended.
And thus we leave the happy pair
to spend their honeymoon in Ayr.

A Nadin

Alas, the marriage was not a success and the couple were eventually to divorce.

With the development of the aeroplane the change from horse and carriage to the motor car also took place. The stables at Hylands were now being used to house the new horseless carriage. Famous names, such as Rolls Royce, Daimler, Rover, Panhard and Renault were at various times kept there.

A 36 h.p. Crossley gas engine and a suction gas plant powering a Crompton's dynamo provided an electricity supply to the house and soon telephone poles were erected across the park to connect the house with communication to the outside world. The present telephone number of the park is derived from the original 'phone number first issued to Hylands at about the beginning of the Great War.

On 26th October Sir Daniel travelled from Buenos Aires with the renowned explorer, Sir Ernest Shackleton [1874-1922], as part of his bid to reach the South Pole. Sir Daniel was one of a curious circle of friends that surrounded Shackleton and he signed before the mast as an Able Bodied Seaman. The second in command, Frank Wild, noted that 'there never was a better A.B. afloat than Sir Daniel Gooch. He obeyed all orders promptly & ... was possessed of a keen sense of humour'.

Sir Daniel's knowledge and expertise with dogs were to keep him in good stead for the voyage to the island of South Georgia, where they arrived on 5th November. Shackleton's ship, *Endurance*, sailed south on 5th December, 1914, but without Sir Daniel.

The reason was that, back in Europe, the Great War had broken out and Sir Daniel received news that Hylands was to be taken over and used as an emergency hospital. He decided to return home to supervise and to fund a hospital equipped with the most technically advanced medical equipment that money could buy. Nothing was too good for the 1,500 patients, known to the locals as 'Blue Boys', who were to be treated there from its opening on 14th August, 1914. The 2nd & 3rd South Midland Ambulance ran two wards of 95 beds.

In retrospect Sir Daniel's was a wise decision, as this was to be the last voyage of the *Endurance*. Sir Ernest and his crew were to be marooned in the inhospitable wilderness of the Antarctic when the ship was caught, crushed and sunk by the pack ice. The crew then resorted to hauling Endurance's small boats that had been saved across the ice until open water was found and then sailing back to South Georgia and safety.

On 14th October, 1914, Lady Gooch was honoured with a visit by King George V, who had come to inspect 15,000 Territorials of the South Midland Division, who had assembled from their billets in and around Chelmsford. Travelling from London in a powerful motor car his arrival at 11.15 caused quite a stir. The crowd was surprisingly large, considering that it was only announced the day before that the King was to come.

Accompanied by General Sir Ian Hamilton the Commander in Chief Home Forces, and Major-General Heath, Colonel Clark and other officers, the march past began with the

King George V being driven through Writtle, having completed his inspection of the troops, 1914

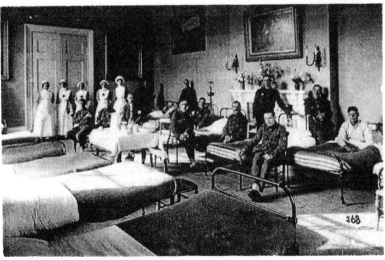

Ward B, ground floor, Hylands, October, 1914

Bedfordshire Yeomanry, the Royal Artillery, the infantry units and the Royal Engineers, followed up by the Cyclists' Corps. The plan to continue to Colchester was abandoned and the King in his motor car left via the Writtle entrance to lunch with the Right Honourable Mark Lockwood, MP, and his wife at their home, Bishop's Hall at Lambourne.

Lord Horatio Herbert Kitchener [1850-1916] visited Hylands on 6th August, 1915, arriving promptly at 11 o'clock to inspect the 2/lst South Midland Division. He was accompanied by General Sir Leslie Rundle and the Commander of the Division, the Marquis of Salisbury. Despite the occasional heavy shower of rain, Lord Kitchener sat on a large white horse whilst the troops marched past him for some 70 minutes. A small aeroplane made a brief appearance and circled overhead. The large crowd of people from Chelmsford and nearby villages filled a large area of the park, eager to see the hero of Khartoum. After the march past Lord Kitchener made a short visit to the hospital wards in the house, before leaving for London via the Writtle entrance.

Two fêtes were held at Hylands, helping to raise over £1,000 for the Essex Regiment's Prisoner of War Fund.

Lancelot Daniel Edward Gooch, Sir Daniel's eldest son, had joined the Royal Navy, but was taken ill while serving on HMS *Implacable*, and died in Greece on 4th October, 1915. A memorial stone was erected in the churchyard at St Mary's, Widford.

The hospital closed in early 1919 and a armistice and demobilization dance was held at Hylands to celebrate.

On 7th September, 1920, the estate was put up for sale, but, having no suitable purchaser, it was withdrawn at £117,000. Eventually a buyer was found and Sir Daniel moved to Tetchbury Mount, Totton, Hampshire. He was now living within a short distance of Southampton, where he kept his 40 ton yacht, and he was to join the Southampton Yacht Club. Amongst his other great interests were his love of anything mechanical, his breeding of greyhounds and his playing of golf.

Lady May died at 5 p.m. on 26th July, 1921, having been ill for some time. She had been fond of gardening and was renowned for her Pekinese spaniels, one of which had won no less than 75 First Prizes at shows. She was also known for her keen interest in amateur dramatics and had trod the boards in performances in Chelmsford, Colchester and Brentwood. At the west end of the nave of Widford church a commemorative stained glass window was erected in 1922 in memory of May Winifred Gooch and Midshipman L D E Gooch.

The desolate Sir Daniel was left to fend for himself. He had been in ill health for some time and in 1923 was to undergo an operation for the amputation of one of his legs, a false leg being fitted.

At 2 o'clock on 22nd December, 1926, Sir Daniel died at his Hampshire home, having suffered with pneumonia for the previous fortnight. His body was brought back to Essex and was buried at Widford church.

Sir Danial Gooch and members of his family   *Chelmsford Library*

A PRIVATE SYNDICATE

The estate was purchased for the sum of £117,000 by a syndicate of local gentlemen with Mr David Hodge of Widford Hall as Chairman.

Little is known of their activities except that it may have been an attempt to persuade the Essex Agricultural Society to hold the shows on a permanent site. This idea was revived in 1953, when the Society were looking for a site, but they decided on an area at Great Leighs.

The Diamond Jubillee of the Essex Show was held at Hylands on 7th and 8th June, 1922, and, with a warm but breezy couple of days, it was a great success. But the Agricultural Society had decided to keep with the tradition of the Show moving to a different venue around the county every year.

The sale of the Hylands estate by Sir Daniel in 1920 had placed Chelmsford Golf Club in a precarious position and the club decided to purchase the freehold land on which the course stood. Mr Hodge sold that land for £1,600 on 11th May, 1922, and was made an honorary life member as a result of the transaction.

Without a purpose for the estate Mr Hodge and his backers decided to place the Hylands estate back up for sale on 29th June, 1922.

Hylands House, about 1912

HANBURY FAMILY [OWNERS 1922-1962]

John Mackenzie Hanbury was born on 16th March, 1861, his early life being spent at Holfield Grange at Coggeshall. On 11th March, 1907, he married Christine Gibson, eldest daughter of James Gibson of Freshwater, Isle of Wight. They set up home at Great West Hatch at Chigwell, and their only son, John Charles, was born on 23rd November, 1908.

John had experience as a big game hunter and, in 1911, became Chairman of the brewers, Truman's, just as Arthur Pryor had been. In August, 1922 John Mackenzie Hanbury bought Hylands for £17,500, but did not purchase all the outlying farms and estates that were also put up for sale. Before he could realise his ambitions for the estate he was to die suddenly on 20th April, 1923, in London. His funeral was held at East Barnet parish church, leaving his widow, Christine and their son, John, to continue living at Hylands. In his will he left £138,752.

Christine was not to vegetate in her loneliness and was soon to prove herself in business, long before the days of women's lib. She was soon running the estate and was elected to the board of Truman's. Lady directors were by no means usual at that time, Christine being selected solely for her proficiency in business matters. She had a reputation for never doing anything by halves and her involvement in the licensed trade was no exception, leading to her becoming President of the Beer & Wine Trade Benevolent Association. She brought elegance and a brand of shrewd common sense that was uniquely her own.

In the late 1920s Christine had constructed a terrace along the back of the house, as well as the ha-ha to replace the remnants of Repton's fencing: the ha-ha can still be seen though it has had to be rebuilt due to soil subsidence. Tennis courts were laid and rhododendron borders planted to the rear lawn, beautifying the garden, but partially screening the view of the park and lake from the house.

In 1927 a plantation of trees behind Boreham House, on the far side of Chelmsford, were felled; the grey herons that

79

The pleasure grounds in the 1930s

The interior of the greenhouse, converted into a swimming pool. The pool still exists, with an islet in the middle, but the greenhouse is long gone.

had nested there were forced to move; they seem to have chosen one of a large group of trees in Hylands Park and, although winter and wind have decimated their number on many occasions, they continue to breed there. By 1961 some 28 breeding pairs were noted, although their numbers are dwindling now.

Christine was eager to share her great possessions with as wide a group of people as possible. One of the ways of doing this was by allowing voluntary organisations the use of Hylands. A society she was particularly closely associated with was the Essex branch of the British Red Cross Society and this led to several big rallies and the visit to Hylands of several distinguished guests.

Before and during the First World War Christine had personally trained many members of the Red Cross detachments, being an authority on both nursing and administrative matters. In 1924 there was a rally and parade of Red Cross personnel, taking advantage of the vast expanse of the rear lawns. The guest of honour was the Lord Lieutenant, Lord Amelius Lambourne [1847-1928], who had visited as Mark Lockwood, MP, a few years earlier, who presented awards to winners of the first aid competitions from the terrace.

On 23rd and 24th May, 1928, the Essex Show was held in the grounds of Hylands for a second time. They were a wet and cheerless couple of days, successful though the Show was. Mr R H Currie was the tenant of the land on which the Show was held.

The Red Cross rally of 2nd June, 1934, received an even greater honour in the form of a visit by Victoria Alexandra Alice Mary, the Princess Royal. In the *Essex Chronicle* it was reported that:

Her Royal Highness the Princess Royal, Commander in Chief of the British Red Cross Society, honoured the Essex branch of the Society and Order of St John of Jerusalem on Saturday by her presence at the annual county rally and fête at Hylands, Chelmsford, the residence of Mrs J M Hanbury, RRC, vice-chairman of the county committee. Glorious sunshine favoured the Royal visit, and the charming grounds and gardens of Hylands provided a perfect setting for the proceeding. The Princess Royal received a great welcome from the nurses and members of the men's detachments, the county and military representatives, and the large attendance of the general public. Her Royal Highness was obviously much impressed by the fine reception, and by all she saw in the efficiency and excellent turn-out of one of the best parades of Voluntary Aid Detachments that has ever been organised in the county.

The Princess Royal, wearing her uniform as Commander in Chief, and accompanied by a lady-in-waiting, also in uniform, journeyed from London to Hylands by motor car, arriving shortly before 4pm. The car was preceded through Essex by two police motor cycle patrols.

Upon the tunic of the Princess were two rows of ribbon decorations, and two medals, including the Royal Red Cross. On the steps of the mansion to greet the Princess were the Lord Lieutenant of Essex, Brig-General R B Colvin, CB, Lady Gwendoline Colvin, CBE, President of the Essex Red Cross Society and chairman of the Rally Committee; the High Sheriff of Essex. Lieut.-Col. E N Buxton, MC; Mrs J M Hanbury; Mr J C M Hanbury; Major General Marshall, GOC, East Anglian Division; Major General F G Fitzgerald, DDMS, Eastern Command; Sir Edward Stewart; Dame Beryl Oliver, from the London Headquarters of the British Red Cross Society. Her Royal Highness often paused to express her admiration and her first remark on returning to the mansion was, "Essex is really a lovely county".

Hylands was, in 1935, considered, amongst other places, as a possible home for what is now called the Writtle Agricultural College, but was rejected as being unsuitable.

In the 1930s the main London road was being converted to dual carriageway and so the brick wall put up by Attwood was demolished. The contractors intended to replace the wall with an inferior fence, but Christine would have none of it. Christine told the contractors, "You take a wall down and you'll put a wall back."

Meanwhile, the Hanbury son, John, known as Jock, having left Eton, had taken his place in the family business. His cheerful disposition and his active interest in the well being of his fellow workers made him a popular member of the firm.

He was an active sportsman, who abandoned traditional hunting in favour of stalking. It gave him great pleasure to initiate his friends into this sport, particularly in the Forest of Loch Rosque. He had met his future wife, Felicity, in 1933 on

Mrs Christine Hanbury
photographed by
Frederick Spalding
Chelmsford Library

John Charles Hanbury

the cruise shiop *Orontes* and they married in 1935 and decided to take flying lessons together at Heston Aerodrome. Together they flew regularly to Le Tocquet for weekends.

It was natural that he should be one of the earliest recruits to the Auxiliary Air Force and soon rose to the rank of Pilot Officer: when the Second World War began P.O. John Charles Hanbury, 90893, was attached to 615 (County of Surrey) Squadron, based at RAF Kenley. Felicity had meanwhile joined No. 9 (City of London) RAF Company of ATS, affiliated to 601 Squadron.

He was one of the first R.A.F. pilots to die, when his Gloster Gladiator II flew into the ground at Holmwood Common, Surrey, whilst on night flying patrol on 1st October, 1939. His ashes were buried in a specially consecrated plot of ground in Hylands Park, along with those of his father.

This second personal tragedy in her life did not cause Christine to give in to a life of self pity. Instead, she found comfort in wholehearted devotion to the care of others. She organised the Essex branch of the joint war organisation prisoner of war department. Between 1939 and 1945 she was the Assistant County Director of the Red Cross.

During the war Hylands was a command post for the military forces, the Commander of the 6th Anti-Aircraft Division (Territorial Army) used the cellars as air raid shelters and also set up wireless communication centres in the basement rooms. The Brigade Commander was Major-General Frederick Gordon Hyland [1888-1962]: who says the military have no sense of the ridiculous!

Fighter pilots of the aerodrome at North Weald and their friends were to be regular users of the swimming pool in the garden.

On 29/30th January, 1944, during sporadic raids over central and southern parts of Essex, a 50kg bomb was dropped 250 yards north of Hylands park. Heinkel 177s of 3/KG100 and 1/KG40 had taken off from their base at Rheine and roamed all over the south-east of England that night and probably one of them was responsible for dropping a stick of bombs that ran from Writtle to Galleywood: the bomb was safely dealt with by a bomb disposal team a few days later.

German PoWs, whose camp was at the northern entrance of the park, were used to cultivate the land on the surrounding farms, but were not allowed near the house.

1944 was to bring a new and very special and secretive force to Hylands. The Special Air Service (S.A.S.) had been set up in the Western desert where they had received their baptism of fire. Early in May, 1944, small groups of men were transferred from bases in North Africa to Darvel, Ayrshire, and Nettlebed, Hampshire and then on to their new forward headquarters in Hylands.

Officers were billeted in the main house, in parts that were not occupied by Christine. The enormous bedrooms could accmmodate up to ten men in each room. Lt-Col 'Paddy' Blair Mayne, DSO [3 bars] was one such officer who was much taken by Christine Hanbury and she was often invited to visit the mess and would hold court there, swirling her long string of pearls, and telling them of her adventures when she had travelled around the world. Christine had a great sense of humour and cheerfully accepted their presence, as they swarmed over the estate she regarded it as, 'doing her bit at dethroning that man, Hitler'.

In a letter to his mother 'Paddy' wrote of her invitation to dinner one night; even with rationing Christine had managed to get a venison roast, red wine, good port and a fine cigar to finish.

Many of the operations undertaken by the SAS were planned from Hylands and all personnel due to be dropped behind enemy lines were taken to the 'Cage' at Fairford, Gloucestershire, where they were briefed and then taken to their aircraft. Dozens of Nissen huts were built to accommodate the SAS squadrons and their administration offices. Between the dual carriageway of the London road and under the large trees that were once part of the estate, the army kept, under camouflage, a great many guns, ammunition and all manner of military equipment.

With the end of the War in May, 1945, the two SAS regiments were used to disarm German forces in Norway, but

Mrs Hanbury and the SAS

Princess Margaret at Hylands,
June, 1949
Chelmsford Library

this was simply to delay what the Army termed 'suspended animation' of the regiments. On their retuirn to Hylands, all that remained was a series of parties and fun and games. One night when Christine had retired, Paddy had for a bet attempted to drive a jeep up the main marble staircase, on to the landing and through the oak doors. Woken by the commotion and suitably attired, Christine appeared on the landing and remonstrated with him for waking her from her slumbers. Paddy, now suitably chastened and full of apologies, dismissed the crowd of onlookers and gallantly escorted her to her bedroom door and bade her 'goodnight'. The jeep was to removed in the morning, but in the cold light of dawn it was to prove impossible to get the vehicle back through the doors. Despite the expertise of the best drivers, this farce concluded by removing the doors from their hinges, but how they got it around the two right-angled bends and through the double front doors of the house is not recorded.

One day Paddy ordered the adjudant to 'phone Chelmsford Fire Brigade and tell them to send an engine, as they had a problem. The brigade assumed there was a fire and sent a fire chief and full crew immediately. On arrival they were met by an astonishing sight. All the mess waiters were lined up in front of the house bearing trays of drinks. Somehow word of this party got back to the fire station and soon the entire Chelmsford force was sitting on the steps supping pints of ale. Thankfully, there were no fires that evening!

On 8th October, 1945, the 1st and 2nd Regiments of the Special Air Service, as well as its Brigade Headquarters, were disbanded and, at a small ceremony at Hylands, attended by Field-Marshal Bernard Montgomery, Paddy made a speech noting that, "We all came for the pillage, but maybe got a wee bit of glory as well." The regiment was to be resurrected and the rest is history.

With the coming of peace Christine resumed her pre-war duties and, as she was twice President of the Essex Agricultural Society, it was not surprising that the park would be used for local organisations and so the Essex Show was held at Hylands on 14th May, 1946. Over 20,000 people attended, but due to the appalling weather it was recorded as the muddiest ever! Christine's dauntless spirit must have been severely put to the test, to say nothing of the patience of her staff, who knew they would have to get the park back into condition afterwards, especially when some 3,500 cars had been churning up the ground.

But apart from a few special occasions, such as a Conservative rally in May, 1948, the park began to become less well looked after, as costs were rising.

A year later Hylands was again honoured with a royal visit, brought about by Christine's interest in the Girl Guide movement. The occasion was the 40th birthday of Essex Guides and the salute was taken by Princess Margaret on 25th June, 1949.

The Princess was at that time the most talked about teenager in Britain and thousands of people gathered to see what she was really like, only to find her a slight figure, shorter than many of the guides she was inspecting. Although she rarely laughed, she was usually smiling. A saluting base had been erected beneath the portico. The relationship between the Princess and Lady Baden-Powell was cordial and, during the march past, at which the Princess was taking the salute, she was talking to Lady Baden-Powell a great deal, thus missing four salutes.

The government's scheme for a university for Essex had been in the air for some time and, as Christine had been a member of the Essex Education Committee, she was eager for Hylands to be the site for the new University of Essex and on 13th April, 1960, she announced that she was prepared to sell Hylands as the University site. It was the first choice of the local University Promotion Committee, but the University Grants Committee decided it was too near London to develop its own academic identity and they preferred Wivenhoe Park, near Colchester.

During her life Christine had kept fit and had visited many parts of the world, including a round-the-world trip, but she was to suffer from arthritis during her later years.

When Christine died on 12th May, 1962, aged 89, no

The Main Staircase (up which the jeep was driven), 1948

The Main Staircase, 1988

specific proposals for Hylands' future existed, though Christine's wishes were known. The estate was inherited by three nieces, all of whom had homes of their own, in Surrey, Devon and France.

A memorial service was held at Writtle church on 29th May and, after cremation, Mrs Hanbury's ashes were interred in the same consecrated plot as the remains of her husband and son. The simple inscription reads, "Christine MacKenzie Hanbury. Born April 4, 1873 - died May 12, 1962, at rest in the garden she loved."

A portrait by Sir James Gunn, RP [1893-1964], of Christine Hanbury now hangs in the boardroom of Truman, Hanbury and Buxton in London.

While the future of the property was in doubt, Mrs Hanbury's butler and his wife lived in the house, acting as caretakers and showing around representatives of various organisations who were showing an interest in its purchase. During this time, on Wednesday, 22nd May, 1963, a fire broke out in the west wing. The Fire Brigade was quickly on the scene, engines coming from as far afield as Great Baddow, Ingatestone, Hatfield Peverel and Basildon. The fire was soon brought under control, but smoke and flames continued to belch from the roof for some time. Much of the stored furniture was badly damaged and thousands of gallons of water cascaded down into the hall and lower rooms. This fire and subsequent water damage were to be responsible for the accelerated rate of decay in this wing.

On 13/14/15/16th July, 1964, Strutt & Parker, estate agents, put the sale of furniture and other furnishings for auction. The house and park were also on offer, but were later withdrawn. In January, 1965, the executors of Mrs Hanbury's will decided to put Hylands House up for sale.

Following the notification of the sale of the Hylands estate by the agents, Strutt & Parker, Lofts & Warner, a Joint meeting was held at County Hall on 30th March, 1965, between Chelmsford Borough, Chelmsford Rural District and Essex County Councils to discuss the possible purchase of the estate. At the conclusion of the meeting it was announced that Chelmsford Borough Council would buy the park and Essex County Council the house: the Rural District Council would not participate, but would hold a watching brief. Eventually Essex County Council were to withdraw as they were unable to find a financially viable use for the property, so leaving Chelmsford Borough Council to purchase the whole estate.

The Borough had for some considerable time wished to conform to the recommendations of the Physical Training and Recreation Act of 1937 and buying the estate would enable the council to reach the recommended figures. This imminent purchase was quickly to bring several enquiries, mainly concerning the lease of the house and parts of the estate. Amongst those applying were Harlow College and Hyde School, who wanted to lease the house and 24 acres of land, Mrs A Mallinson who wanted to lease the house and 18 acres for a girls' school, King Edward Grammar School in Chelmsford who wanted to lease 25-30 acres for playing fields, and from Chelmsford Cricket Club to lease 10-12 acres.

Loan sanction from the government was granted in November, 1965, and, with negotiations completed with the estate agents, the final Purchase of the estate by Chelmsford Borough Council was made on 2nd April, 1966, for the sum of £150,000. A further £3,600 was spent by the council that year on painting the house and on some renovation work. And so, on 6th May, 1966, the Park was officially opened to the public for the first time.

When the council took over the park some parts of the gardens were quite overgrown, but the Parks Department employees, some of whom had worked for Mrs Hanbury, began to bring the park back to former glories, although some buildings on the estate had already disappeared and some more were later to be demolished.

The house itself was already in the grip of progressive decay and dilapidation. The long period while the house had been unoccupied combined with closed windows and doors, preventing proper ventilation, had encouraged the growth of dry and wet rot spores behind plasterwork and wood panelling. In 1966 a council estimate for repairs to the house totalled £3,000 for dealing with dry rot and roof repairs.

Further ideas proposed for the park included a racecourse, while the Curator of the Chelmsford and Essex Museum proposed the use of 11.85 acres of Home Farm and a paddock for an outdoor museum of Essex Town and Country Life. On 14th September, 1966, the Metropolitan Police Mobile Training Column used part of the park for their civil defence training. and during the summer months the Salvation Army band performed concerts; in the autumn a lorry load of dead wood was collected and distributed by the Round Table to local pensioners for the oncoming winter.

In 1967 the house was placed on the list of houses of historic or architectural merit by the government and was listed as being Grade II. During a stormy four-hour Council Meeting in January, 1967, a proposal for a 18 hole golf course covering 123 acres, was made to the Council by Mr John Sherman, the Borough Council's Parks Director. The plan included an archery green, boating, angling, a camping site, stables for horse riding, a children's playground including a model railway, etc. The project was scrapped later that year.

Rentokil, Ltd. estimated that some £2,360 work needed to be done, after an inspection of the house in February, 1967, but no work was carried out, and a further £500 estimate in March to eradicate dry rot was not completed until roof repairs were made, only after which could any work proceed.

The B B C wrote to the Council asking to use the outside of the house for filming on 7th/8th March, 1967, at ten guineas a day.

John Richmond's clock above the stable block had stopped and inquiries were made about its repair and renovation. It was cleaned and repaired to full working order by the Chelmsford Model Engineering Society by January, 1971.

A café was proposed for the gardener's bungalow, which could then be leased out each summer, but this was not acted upon. Meanwhile the clearance of overgrown areas of the park was voluntarily undertaken by the Chelmsford and District Youth Leaders' Council. A request was made to clean out and restock the lake.

By October, 1967, councillors recommended that a 'final' decision on the use of the house should be made. The only final decision was on Southwood Cottage, which was in a poor state of repair and so, during the winter of 1967, it was demolished by Messrs. Sherman Bros. The Council refused permission for a local hunt in April, 1968.

The Chelmsford Silver Band performed in the park during the summer and a camping display by the 24th Chelmsford Scout Troop was held. In June a Horse Show and Gymkhana was held in the park. Alderman Ted Wilkes, the Mayor of Chelmsford, held a Mayor's garden party on the rear lawn on 18th July, while at a full Council Meeting that month it was decided to ban the public from practising golf in the park.

Mr R A Boxall in his report to the Council in July, 1968, estimated that the cost of repairs had risen to £97,000: Rentokill's earlier estimate for work was not accepted.

Writtle Parish Council approached Chelmsford to lease part of the Shakestone plantation, bordering on to Writtle's playing field, for use as a playground.

A small realignment of the estate boundary with land belonging to Mr P A Day was completed on 15th August, 1969. Permission was given for Broomfield College to start a nature trail and, in September, 1969, a horse trial was held by the East Essex Horse Society in the park. The suggestion by Eric O Reed, Chelmsford's Borough Librarian and Curator of the Chelmsford & Essex Museum, for turning Home Farm into an industrial museum was considered.

In September, 1969, thieves stripped lead off the roof, resulting in rain penetration.

The Eastern Sports Council's *Golf Report*, dated June,

The drawing room and south-east room, 1988

1970, recommended that a comparable golf course for a park like Hylands would cost £60-65,000 for the course, plus £30,000 for club houses and £3,500 for parking. Chelmsford Council's Finance Committee voted to demolish the House that same month, as some seven months previously it had been estimated that some £153,000 would be needed for restoration. Essex County Council was opposed to demolition, according to an article in the *Essex Chronicle* of 15th January, 1971.

Dry rot in the servants' quarters was diagnosed and in June, 1971, after obtaining listed buildings consent, the demolition of the domestic offices between the house and the stables took place, being completed by 25th August, 1971. An application by the Council for listed building consent for the demolition of the first floors of the wings was granted by the Department of the Environment, but not proceeded with.

Grant funds are always limited and are thus allocated to the greatest need, the architectural merit and historical importance and, although the government did recognise Hylands as being of sufficient merit, it could not offer such a large grant as was envisaged.

The possibilities of an open air theatre, with part of the house being incorporated into the design, were talked of in July, 1971.

The access to the park was via Paradise Road and, due to the narrowness of the carriageway, caused a great deal of anguish to drivers and residents alike. To try to solve the problem the Eastern National Omnibus Company was asked to provide a public bus service, but their vehicles were unable to easily negotiate Paradise Road. However, Wells Coaches of Hatfield Peverel, with their smaller coaches, could and so a three year contract was signed for a service to run from the Civic Centre in Chelmsford, starting on 4th July, 1971. The demand was not sufficient and the service folded as the Council was not disposed to subsidise the undertaking.

In the summer of 1971 Hylands Development Committee was set up by the council; a safari across all parts of the park and into the house was made by committee members on 30th January, 1972, and a final report was published that August.

A Pageant of Song, Music and Dance was held in May, 1972, by the Chelmsford and District Community Association.

A move to demolish the entire house was made in the Council Chamber during a difficult 3 hour meeting in October, 1972, but was defeated by 15 votes to nine. A vote was made not to proceed with the intention of making 117 acres into a golf course by 16 to 10: Home Farm was now facing demolition, which was approved by the Council and carried out by Messrs Sherman Bros.

On 22nd October, 1972, a large piece of the parapet and cornice fell from the west wing of the house, due to water penetration, and so timber shoring was erected to support the outer wall. A call to preserve the portico and part of the house, with the balance being demolished, thus leaving just a façade, was made in 1973. The report, published in December, 1974, was not acceptable to the public or Councillors, who disliked the recommendations.

Period & Country Homes, owned by Christopher Buxton, entered into discussion with the Council about converting the house into five flats on the first and second floors and renovating the ground floor; an offer of £195,000 was discussed. Period & Country Homes and Baker's of Danbury were invited to submit fixed price tenders for this conversion. By March, 1973, the price of Hylands had risen to £287,000.

The local government re-organisation of 1974, halted any progress for a while, but plans were talked of for a motor museum. A suggestion that Prince Charles might wish to reside at Hylands was turned down. An Agricultural Show was held by the Federation of Young Farmers that year and a caravan rally was held on August Bank Holiday.

To improve the security of the house a 1.8 metre high chain link fence was to surround the house during the autumn of 1974, protecting the public from the possibility of falling masonry and protecting the house from petty vandals. The possible re-opening of the A12 access to the park was broached to the government, but turned down.

Two proposals for the house were put forward, including one by the Council itself; these were for the preservation of the portico only, while the other was for the preservation of the portico and entrance hall only, at a cost of £43,000 and £108,000 respectively (including professional fees). Both schemes were rejected at a Council Meeting in January, 1975.

In February, 1975, the Council decided to demolish the house - a decision that was to earn them the title of 'Vandals of the Year'.

The house was upgraded in 1975 to Grade II* in the list of buildings of architectural or historical interest. The head gardener's bungalow was demolished that summer. Within the park the all-too-prolific grey squirrels had to be culled.

Period and Country Homes ended their negotiations with the Council as the potential rate burden would be too high. In November, 1975, the council considered a development report which again included a golf course.

Following listed building consent that had been applied for in 1975, a public enquiry was ordered for 17th January, 1976. The enquiry, chaired by Mr Ramsay Chase, was scheduled for three days, but was to last for nearly three weeks.

Chelmsford Borough representatives put forward the case for demolition, while the case against was led by Essex County Council, with the Chelmsford Society, the Chelmsford Chapter of Architects, the Ancient Monuments Society, the Essex Archæological Society, the Essex Archæological and Historical Congress, the Garden History Society, the Georgian Society and the Victorian Society. Mrs Eleanor Burgess, a Chelmsford Councillor, and Mr Frank Cooper, the headmaster of Chelmer Valley High School, Chelmsford, made personal representations against the demolition.

Had restoration been undertaken in 1966 it would have cost £60,000, but inflation over the intervening ten years had now made it an uneconomic proposition. According to the Chartered Surveyor, Mr John Cooper, giving evidence on behalf of the Borough Council, some £777,500 would now have to be spent on restoration and the council would then have a building worth only £300,000 on the open market - clearly an uneconomic proposition. Christopher Buxton, who participated in the enquiry, indicated that he was still interested in the

The main landing, 1988

A bedroom, 1988

house. He and his company were to emerge as probably the best answer to the council's problem of what to do with the house should permission be refused.

In the Chelmsford Arts Festival an illustrated public lecture was given by the Chelmsford Library Players. Jane Dansie wrote a script and, with photographic slides and film, produced a two hour long lecture. Andrew Way, Jane Dansie, Janet Newman, Michael Sayers, Susan Bryett and myself took this lecture to the Christian Centre, Writtle, on 31st March and it was repeated on 7th and 9th April at Christ Church Hall, Chelmsford. It was from this lecture that the idea of the present book was to grow.

On 26th July, 1976, the result of the public enquiry was made known, the report concluding that permission should be refused. The inspector stated that "The demolition of this important house would not be in the public interest and ought to be prevented". He then urged that £50,000 of first aid repairs should be made to make the house safe. He concluded the report saying, 'that it is a fine example of an 18th and mid-19th century house in a finely landscaped park. The house is also important for its fine interiors, and is of historical interest". The council was now faced with an impossible situation: it couldn't demolish the house and it could not afford solely to pay the cost of renovation.

Plans for a Museum of Rural Life were talked of that August. In a report to the council on 30th November, 1976, it was recommended that £14,700 of emergency temporary repairs should be undertaken to deal with spreading dry rot that had been found in the House that April. The work was completed shortly thereafter, except for the west wing, which was dangerous for the workmen to enter.

In 1977 there was once more talk of a golf course for the park, as local estate agents, Munday's of Chelmsford, acting on behalf of a client asked the council to lease the house and part of the park for this purpose, but they were to withdraw over uncertainty about listed building consent.

Essex Young Farmers were to hold a Mudlark Day in the park in May, 1977.

An enquiry from Jason Developments to the council regarding the restoration of the house was made, but progressed no further.

As a result of the public enquiry an estimate for work to eradicate dry rot and to make the building watertight was calculated at £250,000. In October, 1977, thieves took lead from the roof of the stable block.

Following the disposal brief issued by Chelmsford Council in 1978 each of the political parties had their own ideas as to who should take over the renovation and use of the building. The Liberals preferred Christopher G Buxton's Period & Country Homes, who were again showing interest in the house and were willing to have a 99 year lease and to convert the house into luxury flats. The Labour Party liked PIC Installations, who had plans for a £1¼M leisure centre, while the ruling Conservatives were in favour of the construction firm of the Carroll Group of Companies based at Brentwood.

The Writtle Community Association held a fête in the park on 2nd July and on 22nd/23rd July a vehicle rally was held by the local Round Table.

A £4,000 grant for tree planting was received by the Council and some 2,000 trees were planted, with a further 8,000 being needed. Part of South Wood was cleared and replanted under a woodland management scheme grant and the Countryside Commission made a further grant for tree planting of £8,830.

In December, 1978, a disposal brief was produced for any interested parties that were considering taking over the building and a secret committee of Chelmsford Council met in May, 1979, to consider Hylands' future. Negotiations with the Carroll Group of Companies were started in April, 1981, with the house being seen as the new headquarters of the firm. Talks were long and protracted and were to break down in May, 1982, over a large extension where the servants' quarters used to be.

During the long period the house was empty it was prey for unscrupulous people who were set on stripping it of its valuable assets. The lead was taken from the roof, thus

More delapidation, 1988

increasing the deterioration of the interior, and in 1981 an attempt by burglars to remove £1,300 of fixtures was foiled by park staff, but they were too late to prevent the loss of some of the ornate fireplaces.

Negotiations with a local landowner were entered into about the right of access from the Margaretting side of the park in 1974/5 and later in 1980/1, but the landowner was not willing to oblige. As part of the planning permission of 1965 there was a condition that the access from the A12 should stay closed. The Department of Transport was again approached in 1981 to give permission to re-open this access, but this was refused. It was said that when the new Chelmsford by-pass was opened the matter could be re-assessed as the volume of traffic on the road should be much reduced.

The political balance of the Council Chamber was to dramatically change in May, 1982, when the ruling Conservative group was replaced by the Liberals.

Meanwhile, estimates for the renovation of the building were increasing ever upwards and, by 1982, stood at £1M and, by that May, demolition of the house was yet again being seriously considered. In June, a second disposal brief for the house was issued by the council, but with no firm contenders.

Flint Cottage, a listed Grade II building was showing signs of distress and, in August, the 19th century lean-to was demolished and steel strengthening bars were fitted to the cottage.

In October, 1982, a Liverpool consortium was interested in turning Hylands into a casino, hotel and bar. By the next month, four offers were being investigated; the Salix Building Designs and Stuart Estates proposals were not entertained and proposals by Anglia Commercial Properties, and Period & Country Homes were withdrawn after protracted talks.

In April, 1983, Councillor Gibson announced that it was the policy of the Council to demolish the house.

A plan for replacing the stable block was turned down in February, 1984, and plans for a golf course were again discussed the next month, and a feasibility study completed.

The next Budget altered the rules for VAT and it was

feared that this might jeopardise the renovation of the house, but the Historic Buildings and Monument Commission came to the rescue with a grant of £250,000.

St John's Church, Moulsham, held a Mardi Gras in August, and in September, 1984, proposals were made by W G Crotch & Sons to lease the house. The feasibility study was presented to the Parks Committee on 12th March, 1985. By June, 1985, it was estimated it would cost £442,000 for a golf course and £224,000 for a club house.

In February, 1985, the council started the Hylands House Reinstatement Fund with an initial sum of £250,000 of public money. By this time all attempts at finding a use for the house had come to nothing, but a generous offer from English Heritage that November of a grant up to £195,000 towards the administrative expenses of the renovation of the house. This changed the position and plans were proposed and tenders for the work invited.

A plan for the restoration of the building to its early 19th century form was drawn up under the direction of Mr Esmond Abraham, Chief Architect of Chelmsford Borough Council: Carden and Godfrey were engaged as executive architects for the Stage 1 works, comprising of the structural repairs and external restoration works.

The first stage was to surround the house in scaffolding, completed by Pinewood Scaffolding of East Ham. In January, 1986, listed building consent for the demolition of the *porte cochère* and to rebuild the early 19th century portico were granted by the Department of the Environment.

Work began in January, 1986, by Baker's of Danbury at an approved tender of £411,000. The central block's third storey was removed and an early 19th century hipped and dormered roof restored. The second storey east and west wings and the mezzanine floor were taken down, the west wing staircase was removed and new hipped roofs were built over the existing accommodation. The final cost was £523,184, excluding professional fees.

In April, 1986, an arboretum for the park was announced as a joint venture between Chelmsford Borough Council and

Writtle Agricultural College: over 200 varieties of tree, some donated by Kew Gardens, were to be planted in 34 acres of the park. This project was conceived by Mark Johnson, an arboreculturist, and was implemented by the students under Sandra Nicholson.

While the Chelmsford by-pass was being constructed, another was being built to take the heavy lorries out of Writtle and, as a result, the Writtle Lodge and the main entrance to Hylands park along Paradise Road was to be permanently cut off by the dual carriageway. In 1987 a new access was built off the by-pass to the park.

The ha-ha built by Christine Hanbury in the 1920s was showing signs of structural distress and so, at a cost of £14,100, was re-built by S A Wright in January, 1987.

The Stage 1 of the renovation of the house being complete, work began in September, 1987, for Savills, the estate agents, to release a brochure on behalf of Chelmsford Borough Council asking interested parties for offers for a 125 year lease of the house. Several parties were interested and negotiations were started. Interest was mainly around the notion of a golf course for the park, with a club house centred around the house, the stables or in the old walled kitchen garden. A group of people, mainly from Writtle, who regularly used the park for walking, were outraged at the thought of being bombarded by golf balls as they perambulated the park. An application to the Department of the Environment to investigate Chelmsford Borough Council giving itself planning permission for the golf course was referred to the Department in September, 1987.

Many trees in the park had now passed maturity and were falling down and, in the great storm of October, 1987, many more were lost. To replace a mature oak, chestnut, silver birch, London plane, ash or hornbeam takes many years. Although Repton's *Red book* is not around to give guidance, the council has been replacing missing trees to help nature regain its full beauty for mere humans to enjoy.

Heavy winter rains caused the culverts from the lake to the River Wid to burst, causing flooding of the surrounding land; this had to be renewed at a cost of £49,000.

A council ecological survey was undertaken of the estate and the discovery of a species of dragonfly was expected to stop the plans of the golf course. The Writtle Society welcomed the news that this would delay the council's work. A historic survey was carried out by Chelmsford Borough Museum staff. Within a few months saw a Register of Parks and Gardens of Special Historic Interest published by English Heritage and it included Hylands as a Grade II park. Thus a thorough ecological and historical survey of the park and estate had now been completed and registered for the benefit of all those interested in the future of Hylands.

The council submitted six planning applications for the house, park and for a golf course in March, 1988. The council undertook a feasibility/evaluation exercise of Flint Cottage in the July.

By June, 1988, a list of firms was put together of those who would tender for the first phase of the golf course, with planned work beginning in the spring of 1988. But the Writtle Society referred the matter to the Ombudsman accusing the Council of maladministration, and pending the investigation, the council deferred any decisions. The Ombudsman decided eventually not to investigate further.

On 26th June, 1988, the Ramblers Association used the permissive route of the Centenary Circle for their members.

1988 was the Centenary Year of Chelmsford Borough Council and, to celebrate, a Spectacular was held. On August Bank Holiday Hylands was to be the venue of a series of musical and other events; over 30,000 people were entertained for two days by many notable celebrities, including Humphrey Lyttleton, Helen Shapiro, Alan Price, the Band of the Royal Engineers, the Royal Philharmonic Pops Orchestra and many others. The event finished with a huge firework display.

The increasing use of the Centenary Circle by walkers caused some gates along the eastern boundary to need replacing, at a cost of £365.

The Hylands Spectacular for August Bank Holiday, 1989, was troubled with inclement weather, but, despite this, 20-25,000 people attended, watching stars like Joe Loss, the

Beverley Sisters, D'Oyley Carte Orchestra, the Chris Barber Jazz & Blues Band and the National Youth Jazz Orchestra.

The stage was increased in size, measuring 60 x 56', taking 15 people over five days to construct it. To accommodate the expected numbers of audience, twelve blocks of toilets were erected and some 4,000 toilet rolls used.

The Hylands Working Party of Chelmsford Council selected two firms from the six that were submitted. One has since dropped out, but further negotiations with the remaining companies are awaiting determination. Of the six planning applications for three golf course proposals, two private developers proposals and one of the council's own proposals for change of use of the house for a restaurant, conference centre, etc., awaited a decision by the Secretary of State. A public inquiry, set for February, 1989, was adjourned at the request of Chelmsford Council. This enabled negotiations to continue with the Sue Ryder Foundation, who wanted oermission to turn the house into a nursing home for the elderly and chronically sick.

Chelmsford's Member of Parliament Simon Burns was to ask in the House of Commons, 'Hylands - what is going on?'

The Hylands Spectacular of August, 1990, included displays by members of the English Civil War Society; unfortunately some got carried away in the heat of battle, and were subsequently 'carried away' by ambulances to Broomfield Hospital for their injuries to be seen to. Also attending were favourites from previous years, like the Searchers, Freddie and the Dreamers, the Syd Lawrence Orchestra, and the Fortunes. Attendance numbers were now beginning to rapidly increase and an area of 24 acres was set aside for car parking.

In 1991 some 78 acres of land that adjoined the park to the north, was changed from agricultural use to public open space; this has subsequently been put to grass. The Council announced that plans for a golf course had now been scrapped. That July Councillors and members of the public were invited to view the inside of the house at weekends.

The 4th Chelmsford Spectacular of August, 1991 was held to over 50,000 people attending. The Three Degrees flew in from the USA especially for this event, and a number of favourite 60's stars appeared. The event cost some £200,000 and was now in profit. The 60's night drew some 20,000 people and the Three Degrees night some 12,000.

By November, such was the public's interest that the house was opened up and some 3,000 people saw around the house in four weekends that month. As a result of this, the 'Friends of Hylands' was to be formed.

Proceeds of programmes sold for the 5th Spectacular of August, 1992, were divided equally between the Mayor's Charity Fund and a fund for restoration work on Hylands House. Over 80,000 people attended, with over 40,000 tickets sold in advance. Topping the bill were Michael Ball, Alexander O'Neal, and Gerry and the Pacemakers. One man even flew in from Australia especially to see Michael Ball's show. 25,000 people came for the 60's night and among other events the American Civil War Society put on various displays. High winds damaged the stage and demolished the ACWS tents. It is sad to relate that 64 year old retired milkman, Ronald Rawlings, died of a heart attack during the 60's night.

The 6th Spectacular of 1993 saw the pop band Take That drew an audience of 25,000 screaming teenagers, their fans started turning up to 1½ days early to ensure a good seat. Other notables attending were Montserrat Caballe and the Tschaikovsky Festival Orchestra, and George Benson. The 60's night saw Shakin' Stevens, Showadawaddy, the Searchers and Marmalade. The Trafalgar Gun Company gave demonstrations on how to fire cannon, with the Royal Artillery Motorcycle Display Team giving value for money to the 85,000 people who attended. The Spectacular was to win the entertainment industry's award for Britain's Best Outdoor Event of 1993.

In September, 1993, Councillor Lumley suggested that the house and park be used as a film background, barbecues etc. and in October the council agreed to spend £3m on restoring Hylands. The first phase, costing £433,000, would start in September, 1994, and tenders were sent out the next month. The Dudley Smith Partnership were the chartered quantity

Re-opening, May, 1995

surveyors, along with W S Atkins Property Services of Chelmsford

The Spectacular of August, 1994, now involved over 100 members of the Council's Leisure Department. The American Civil War Society put on displays along with mediæval jousting by Black Knights. Pop bands included Beautiful South, Status Quo, The Royal Philharmonic Orchestra under Cari Davis, with the Searchers and others playing on the ever-popular 60's night.

A change in the marriage laws was to give new impetus for the restoration of the house. No longer would couples have only a choice of either a church or registry office wedding, now they could be held in any place that was officially licensed.

The long awaited rejuvenation of Hylands became reality when the doors of the house were thrown open to the public on a full time basis on 27th May, 1995. Though the house was only partially restored, it showed the public what they wanted to see. The grand entrance hall and an adjoining room had been painstakingly restored, its elaborate sculptured friezes cleaned and the marble effect wall panels and wooden doors restored. The public could now see through glazed screens, those interior rooms that were still waiting restoration. The house, because of its Grade II* listed building status, meant that the council had to comply with strict English Heritage guidelines as to its restoration.

The first phase cost £350,000 including the costs of securing the infrastructure of the building, some £30,000 of this coming as revenue from tickets and programmes sold at the 1994 Spectacular. An entrance fee of £2 to view the interior of the house helping towards the cost of restoration.

There was to be no spectacular for 1995, as this would clash with the nation's tribute to the 50th anniversary of ending of World War Two. Instead, a drumhead service was held on the 20th August, 1995 at 11 a.m. in the presence of the Lord Lieutenant of Essex, with many ex-servicernen's organisations and veterans of World War Two. The Essex Yeomanry Band played and a single Spitfire gave a victory roll over the park.

Re-opening, May, 1995

A report in September, 1995, dealt with the access from the A1016 and the use of the old kitchen garden as a car park. In November a revised layout for the arboretum was put forward which would lessen its impact on the effectiveness on the 'concert bowl' as that area of the park it is called. This layout would take place gradually over a 5-year period.

In February, 1996, a Positive Solution presentation was made by David Fishel as part of market research commissioned by Chelmsford Borough Council and Essex County Council into concepts for the development of cultural and heritage schemes. This focussed mainly on Hylands House and Sandford Mill and was held before a joint Arts and Hylands House sub-committee.

As a precursor to any work being done in the kitchen garden an archæological investigation was undertaken in 1996. Two trenches were excavated, revealing the brick footings of a peach house or vinery of about 1819-25 on the south side of the garden. On the north side of the garden, the footings of a boiler-house were revealed. Many interesting and innovatory aspects were revealed within the walled garden, some being of the earliest of their kind in Britain.

The Hylands Committee met and approved £1.2m to be spent on restoration, but the Labour party objected and called for the money to be spent on a hospice.

Maztech Ltd approached Chelmsford Council to hold a 2-day music concert (17th-18th August, 1996) before the Chelmsford Spectacular. This was the V96 show, sponsored by Virgin Cola to replace the festival usually held at Glastonbury. The show pulled such notable as Paul Weller, Pulp, Supergrass, and Jarvis Cocker to entertain over 70,000 people.

The Spectacular itself (23rd -26th August, 1996) drew over 80,000 on two very hot days. The stars included Boyzone and Lesley Garratt with the Royal Philharmonic Orchestra. A 70's night plus a 60's night drew the people in, on the Monday the Red Arrows put a display on over the park. It was to be voted Best European Festival of the Year by *Live!* magazine.

July, 1997, saw the council agreeing to spend an estimated £1.4m on restoration work on the east wing of the house.

The V97 show held on the 16th-17th August, 1997, drew an audience of over 110,000 fans. Stars such as Addict, Blue Tones, Blur, and Prodigy drew in huge numbers of people, but the subsequent mess had to be quickly cleared up for a Christian Pop Concert held immediately afterwards.

The Spectacular of 21st-22nd, 1997, drew in 80,000 people and over 40 different bands, starring Mike Oldfield, the Sex Pistols, Blur, Peter Andre, Chris de Burgh, and Suzie Quatro, who appeared in the 70's night. The Searchers were among bands in the 60's night, and a special one-off show of *Les Misérables* was staged.

The organiser of these events - Malcolm Gillham, who headed the Council's Leisure Department decided to retire; if anybody deserved a rest he surely did!

Some 66 acres of land lying between Hylands and the Writtle by-pass was bought by the council and has been laid down as pastureland, extending the park even further.

Following an announcement by the Heritage Lottery Fund in March, 1998, of an £18,700 gift towards the Council appointing Scott Wilson Resources as consultants to undertake a feasibility study and to prepare a restoration plan for the entire estate, gardens, the kitchen garden, and buildings such as Flint Cottage, etc. This would enable the council to determine a suitable approach to manage the park and would form the basis for further bids from the Heritage Fund. The report is anticipated being completed by the spring of 1999 for presentation to the Leisure Committee of the council and then to the Heritage Lottery Fund.

The house was again closed to the public as work on East Wing (the second phase) was started by Sindalls of Cambridge, but it would not include the restoration of the grand banqueting room, which will have to wait its turn. This work would bring into public use the four rooms of the East wing at a cost of £1.4m.

The Drawing Room has had conservation work on its detailed ceiling, its wall finishings and the fireplace surround. A large Victorian over-mantle mirror, sold as part of the estate of Mrs Hanbury, has now been put back, a crystal chandelier put up, and furnishings added to allow for appropriate events, including weddings.

The Library has been restored as an exhibition gallery, small-scale function room and alternative room for weddings. The walls and ceiling plaster mouldings and surviving pelmets, along with the fireplace have all undergone conservation.

The adjoining Saloon, which provides wheelchair access to the Drawing Room and Library, has undergone decoration of the Attwood period to match those rooms. The ceiling was rebuilt and new marble fireplaces installed to replace the stolen originals.

The Boudoir Room, that is between the Saloon and the Billiard Room, behind the Entrance Hall, has had double sliding doors added, so linking the two rooms and also matching the decor.

The refurbishment of the former Study Room to provide office space and a temporary storage area under the Drawing Room and Library, the installation of central heating and the restoration of windows in the east wing. Fittings such as pelmets and shutters, which have been in storage for many years, have been renovated and put back into their original places. Marble fireplaces and mirrors have been recreated and put back in place.

Modern oil-fired central heating replaced the Victorian hot air central heating system. These hot pipes are carried around the house in a perimeter trench that will assist the ventilation of the basement and dry out any residual moisture in the brickwork. The excavation of this trench, and for two new basement rooms, was carefully recorded by Essex County Council's Field Archæology Unit. Several unknown walls were discovered including part of the original Georgian basement trench, and part of the curving brick wall that was part of Repton's East wing.

Additional parking spaces have been constructed by Sindall's, near the entrance to the stable block.

During the summer of 1998 an archæological dig was done on the Georgian ice-house in Ice-house Plantation. Long before the refrigerator was invented ice was cut from the nearby pond during the depths of winter and the ice-house filled up; this helped preserve food during the hot summer that would follow. As expected, the domed roof of this structure had collapsed and filled up. One story was that this "collapse" was assisted by the use of plastic explosive during a training session by the Army during the war!

Whilst this work was being done in the house, a programme of events on the rear lawn and gardens was held, such as a performance of *The Taming of the Shrew* between 23-26th July.

The V98 concerts drew over 110,000 people over the 22nd and 23rd August, with 26 arrests being made and 186 people being taken to hospital. Despite a rainy Sunday the crowds gathered to be entertained by the Verve, Underworld, the Charlatans and others.

The Spectacular of August 1998 starred Lesley Garrett and Michael Ball together with the BBC Concert Orchestra. Popular events such as the 60's night, and the American Civil War Society made their usual appearance. Music/Dance shows, such as *Evita* and the *Spirit of the Dance*, drew large numbers, but the draw of large numbers of people also meant large numbers of behind-the-scene workers. This drew the attention of the Customs and Excise, the Inland Revenue, the Contributions Agency and Chelmsford Borough Council to possible fraud perpetrated by people claiming dole money, as a result of which some 20 benefit claims were stopped and 50 investigations begun.

One of the many uses of Hylands House will be as a venue for wedding ceremonies and receptions. As from April, 1999, ceremonies can be held in the Drawing Room, Library, Saloon, the Boudoir Room, or Entrance Hall. Exclusive use of all of the house and grounds for a whole day can be arranged.

The opening of Hylands House at Easter, 1999, sees that Hylands is well on its way to recovery. It is now being put to new and various uses by the people of the area, just as it has throughout its history, recorded in this book. For over two hundred and seventy years the living entity that is Hylands has continued, albeit sometimes battered by nature or man, but now it is recovering to thrive and prosper again and hopefully will continue to do so for a further two hundred and seventy years more....

Those who want to know more about the opening hours of the house or the activities held in and around the house can contact the Hylands House special telephone number (01245) 606812.

View from Passage looking across Entrance Hall to Hall, 1948

Hylands Hall, as restoration started, 1988

Facts and Figures on Hylands Estate

Date of sale particulars	Owner period	Mansion, park, gardens and pleasure grounds		Estate, (including park, woodlands, farms, etc.)	
		Acres	Hectares	Acres	Hectares
Chelmsford Chronicle 31/7/1795	John Richard Comyns 1760-1797	100	40.47	400	161.88
			all approximate		
Chelmsford Chronicle 7/7/1797		121, 1 rod, 4 perches	48.97	438, 2 rods, 3 perches	177.25
Chelmsford Chronicle 7,14,21,28/10/1814	C H Kortright 1797-1815	213	86.2	584	236.34
Chelmsford Chronicle 5/7/1839	P C Labouchere 1816-1839	300 approx.	212.41	750	303.52
22/3/1854	John Attwood 1839-1854	590, 3 rods, 34 perches	239.15	4289,2 rods, 22 perches	1735.73
6/6/1854		549, 2 rods, 15 perches	222.41	1152, 1 rod, 30 perches	466.37
5/12/1854		533, 6 perches	215.7	890, 1 rod, 20 perches	360.32
21/9/1920	Sir D F Gooch 1908-20	479.916	194.22	4011.121	1623.28
29/6/1922	D Hodge 1920-1922	448.269	181.41		
1965	Mrs C Hanbury	432.728	175.12	444.997	180.08
1971-	Chelmsford Borough Council	428 approximately	173	570 approximately	230.68

BIBLIOGRAPHY

Published Books

Abbott, John H. The Courtright (Kortright) Family. Tobias Wright (USA), 1922.

Abraham, Esmond. Hylands: an architectural history. Chelmsford Borough Council, 1988.

Acton, John Emerich Edward Dalbert Acton, Baron. Cambridge Modern History, vol. 9. Cambridge U P, 1906

Addison, William. Essex worthies. Phillimore, 1973

Allen, Cecil J. The Great Eastern Railway. Ian Allan, 1975

Aspinall, A, ed. The later correspondence of George III, vol. 5. Cambridge U.P., 1906

Black Book of Lincoln's Inn, vol. 3. Lincoln's Inn, 1899

Bradford, Roy & Dillon, Martin. Rogue warrior of the S.A.S.: Lt-Col 'Paddy' Blair Mayne. John Murray, 1987

Brayley, Edward Wedlake & Britton, John. The Beauties of England and Wales, vol. 5. Vernon & Hood, 1803.

Buist, Marten G. At spes non fracto: Hope & Co., 1770-1817, merchant bankers and diplomats at work. [The Hague], 1974

Burke's Dormant and Extinct Peerage

Burke's Landed Gentry. Various editions

Burke's Peerage and Baronetage. Various editions

Butler, Iris. The eldest brother: the Marquess Wellesley, 1760-1842. Hodder, 1973.

Carter, George. Humphry Repton, landscape gardener, 1752-1818. Sainsbury Centre for Visual Arts, 1982.

Cole, Hubert. Fouché: the unprincipled patriot. Eyre & Spottiswoode, 1971

Coller, Duffield William. People's history of Essex. Meggy & Chalk, 1861

Colvin, Howard Montague. Biographical dictionary of English architects, 1660-1840. Murray, 1978

Cooper, Johnny. One of the Originals; the story of a founder member of the SAS. Pan, 1991.

Cromwell, Thomas Kitson. Excursions in the County of Essex, vol.1. Longman, 1818.

Dictionary of Architecture, vol.1. Architectural Publication Society Dictionary, Richards, 1852-92

Dictionary of National Biography. Oxford U P, 1912 onwards

Dod's Parliamentary Companion, 1843

Dod's Electoral Facts, 1832-1853

Eastern Counties Railways Act, 1838

Felstead, Alison, etc. Directory of British architects, 1834-1900. Mansell, 1993

Fletcher, Harold Roy. The story of the Royal Horticultural Society, 1804-1968. Oxford U P, 1969

Gash, Norman. Politics in the age of Peel. Harvester, 1977

Gordon, Donald Ian. The eastern counties. 2nd ed. David & Charles, 1977

Johnson, Joan, ed. The General: the travel memoirs of General Sir George Whitmore. Alan Sutton, 1987.

Kelly, Alsion. Mrs Coade's stone. Self Publishing Association, 1990

Kelly's Directory of Essex. Various editions, 1845 to 1937

Lefebvre, George. Napoleon, 1779-1807 & 1807-1815, Routledge, 1969

McHardy, George. Catalogue of the Drawings Collection of the Royal Institute of British Architecti: Office of J B Papworth. Gregg, 1977

Morant, Philip. History and antiquities of the county of Essex. E P Publishing, 1978 (reprint of 1763-8 edition)

Mullman, Peter. A new and complete history of Essex ... by a Gentleman, vol.1. Hassell, 1769-72

Neale, John Preston. Views of the seats of noblemen and gentlemen in England, Wales, Scotland and Ireland. Series1, vol.2. Sherwood, Neely, Jones and Thomas Moule, 1819

Newton, Kenneth Charles. The Manor of Writtle: the development of a royal manor in Essex, c1086-c1500. Phillimore, 1970

O'Leary, J G. The book of Dagenham. 3rd ed. Dagenham Public Library, 1964

Owen, Geoff. Writtle: a village of distinction. Blueprint Pub., 1993

Oxley-Parker, John. The Oxley-Parker Papers. Benhams, 1964

Palmer, Alan. An encyclopaedia of Napoleon's Europe. Weidenfeld, 1984

Peake, Felicity. Pure chance. Airlife Pub., 1993

Pearson, Hesketh. Labby. Hamish Hamilton, 1936

Plon, Eugène. Thorvaldsen: his life and works. Richard Bentley, 1874

Report from the Select Commission on Election Proceedings, 1842

Report of the Commissioner's for Inquiring concerning Charities, 1824-1840

Repton, Humphry. Observations of the theory and practice of landscape gardening. Phaidon Press, 1981 (repr 1803 ed)

Robinson, John. The Attwood family. Hills, 1903

Rush, Joseph Arthur. Seats in Essex. King, Sell, 1897

Sanders, Muriel. Glimpses of Galleywood. Galleywood PCC, 1973

Sargeaunt, John A history of Felsted School. Durrant, 1889

Sedgwick, Romney, ed. The history of Parliament: the House of Commons, 1715-1754, vol.1. HMSO, 1970

Select Committee on the Harwich Election Petition, 1847-8

Shawcross, J P. A history of Dagenham. 2nd ed. Skeffington, 1908

Steer, Francis W. Farm and cottage inventories of mid-Essex, 1635-1749. Phillimore, 1969

Stroud, Dorothy. Humphry Repton. Country Life, 1962

Thorold, Algar Labouchere. The life of Henry Labouchere. Constable, 1913

Truman the Brewers: the story of Truman, Hanbury, Buxton & Co., Ltd. Newman Neame, 1966

Victoria County History of England: Essex, vols 1-8

Warden, Ken. Chelmsford Golf Club, 1893-1993. Chelmsford Golf Club, 1993

Weaver, Leonard T. The Harwich story. Harwich Pr. Co., 1975

White, William. History, gazetteer and directory of the County of Essex. Leader, 1848 and (2nd ed) 1863

Who's Who of British Members of Parliament. Harvester, 1976-81

Wilde, Mrs E E. Ingatestone and the Great Essex Road. Milford, 1913

Wright, Thomas. History and topography of the County of Essex, vol.1. Virtue, 1836

Wright, Thomas. The picturesque beauties of Great Britain. G Virtue, 1831

Ziegler, Philip. The sixth great power: Barings, 1762-1929. Collins, 1988

Printed Material

Beadel, estate agents. Particulars of a very valuable residential estate known as Hylands Park ... Sale particulars, 6th June, 1854

Catalogue of the unreserved sale of the furniture, sculpture, books and other effects at 'Hylands Park' , late the

residence of John Attwood, Esq. August, 1854

Chelmsford Borough Council. Hylands House, 1982

Chelmsford District Council. Hylands: report on proposed scheme for preservation of portico and part of south-west front, 1974

Chelmsford Society. Hylands House... proposals for the restoration and development of the house for public use, 1979

Dansie. Jane. Hylands: family home for 200 years. Script of lecture given by the Chelmsford Library Players, 1976

Knight, Frank & Rutley. Hylands House Sales Particulars, 7th September, 1920

Papworth, Wyatt. John B Papworth: a brief record of his life and works. Privately published, 1879

Richman, Harry. Billericay and its High Street. C P R E (Billericay Group), 1953

St Mary's Church, Widford. Centenary, 1862-1962

Savills of Chelmsford. Sale catalogue of Leasehold of Hylands House, 1987

Should there be a public golf course in Hylands Park? Chelmsford Council, 1965

Upton, J H. A history of Writtle church in the county of Essex. Privately published, 1930

Valuable printed books, historical documents, manuscripts, autograph letters and maps ... to be sold at auction on 14th February, 1980, by Lawrence of Crewkerene

Van Den Muijzenberg, Erwin W B. A history of greenhouse. Institute for Agricultural Engineering, Netherlands, 1980

Newspapers and Periodicals

Architectural History. Vol.28. 1985, p71-101. Kelly, Alison: Coade stone in Georgian architecture

Architectural Preservation. Vol. 1, no. 3, Autumn, 1982, p.23. New use sought for Hylands House, Writtle, near Chelmsford

Building Design. 28 February, 1975, p16. O'Connery, C: Death of a mansion: Hylands House

Building Design. 7 May, 1976, p28. Boutwood, James: Death by Public Enquiry

Chelmsford Chronicle (later Essex Chronicle), 1764 onwards

Country Life. Vol.151, p928. Hopes from a Georgian mansion

Country Life. 19 December, 1985, p1996-7. Abraham, Esmond: Ghostly fingerprints: Humphry Repton and Hylands

Country Life. 27 January, 1983, p186-8. Laing, Alistair: Clubhouse neoclassicism: sculpture at Stoke Poges

Dagenham Digest, the quarterly journal of the Borough. No.55, April, 1962, p455-7. Judge Sir John Comyns

Essex Herald, 1800-1943

Essex Journal. Vol.17, pt3, p9. Tritton, P: Nine to five [Widford siding in 1882]

Essex Review. 1892 to 1957

Essex Review. Vol.58, p43. Emmison, F G: Hylands

Essex Review. Vol.49, p43. Hills, Alfred: The Hanbury armorial china
Essex Weekly News. 1862 onwards
Friends of Blue. Bulletin no. 28, Winter, 1982-3, p. 3. Otto, Doreen. Crown Acorn
and Oak Leaf Border Series
Friends of Blue. Occasional papers. No. 1, Spring, 1990. Otto, Doreen. John Meir
of Tunstall and the Impressed Crown
Gardener's Chronicle. 11 June, 1881, p763
Gardener's Magazine. Vol.4, 1838, P633-4. Ferguson, J A: List of ligneous plants
which have stood the winter of 1837-8 at Highlands near Chelmsford, Essex
Gardener's Magazine.   March, 1828, p385-400.   Some account of the Dutch
manner of forcing, as practiced in the kitchen-garden at Hylands, near
Chelmsford, the seat of P C Labouchere, Esq., F.H.S.
Gentleman's Magazine. 1731 to 1868
Gloucester Journal. 1818
Hugenot Society's Proceedings. vol.10, no .1, p176-7. The Labouchere pedigree
Peacock's Polite Repository. May, 1804. Engraving by J Peltro from a miniature
sketch of Hylands by Humphry Repton
Revue d'Histoire Diplomatique. 1913, p425-55. Labouchere, George: Un financier
diplomatique au dernier siècle: P C Labouchere
Transactions: Essex Archaeological Society. 3rd series, vol.8, p292. Tritton, P: A
clue to the Anglo-Saxon watermill
Transactions of the Horticultural Society of London.   Vol.7, 1828, p400-2.   An
account of a cherry orchard at Hylands, near Chelmsford, the seat of P C
Labouchere, Esq., F.H.S.

Unpublished notes and muscripts
Estate papers of the Hylands Estate [E.R.O. D/DHyl
Holman, William. Manuscript note on the history of Essex [Writtle and Widford]
Parish registers of Writtle [E.R.O. D/P 50], Widford [E.R.O. D/P 244, Chelmsford
EE.R.O. D/P 94], Aston, Hertfordshire
Trow, Helen. History of Widford. Emmison Essay entry, 1962 [E.R.O. T/Z 13/73]
Will of John Richard Comyns 1799 [E.R.O. 233 BR 29]

Hylands in 1770   Chelmsford Library

Hylands, 1831, drawn by William Henry Bartlett

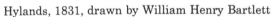

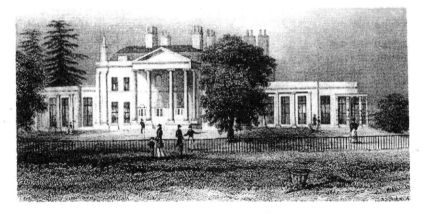